Techniques of Investigation:

an introduction to research methods

NEC
NATIONAL
EXTENSION
COLLEGE

National Extension College
18 Brooklands Avenue
Cambridge
CB2 2HN

© 1992 National Extension College Trust Ltd.

First printed 1992
Revised 1993 for use with Judith Bell, *Doing your Research Project*, Open University Press (1993, 2nd edition)

ISBN 1 85356 153 3

Compiled by: Linda Deer Richardson
Page layout by: Mary Bishop
Cartoons by: Eric Jones
Printed by: NEC Print

Acknowledgements
We are grateful to the following copyright holders for permission to include extracts from other sources as follows:

Judith Bell and Open University Press for quotations from Judith Bell (1993) *Doing Your Research Project* , Open University Press: as acknowledged in the text.

Judith Bell (and University of Sheffield) for extracts from *Module Three: Methods of Educational Enquiry*, a course prepared for the University of Sheffield Division of Education Distance Learning Programme, and, like this one, using *Doing Your Research Project* as its set text. Material adapted for use in this course is as follows:

Unit 1:	Chart from p. 5; material from paras 1.3 and 1.6, 1.9, 1.10.
Unit 2:	List of topics from Para 2.3. Activity 3 based on paras 2.6–2.10. Activity 7 based on para 2.18.
Unit 3:	Paras. 3.8–3.9. Activity 4 based on para 3.4.
Unit 4:	Paras 4.5, 4.6, 4.9, 4.11, 4.12, 4.15.
Unit 5:	Paras 5.6–5.9, 5.15, 5.18–20.
Unit 9:	Paras 8.2–8.6.
Unit 10:	Paras 9.3–9.5.
Part 3:	Introduction uses Paras 10.1–3; 10.11–14.
Unit 11:	Para 10.4.

YMCA National College for extracts from the Diploma of Higher Education: Informal Education, by distance learning (prepared by the compiler and other members of the Course Team):

Unit 1:	Material on purpose/audience action and broad/narrow scope research from *Individuals* 7/1, 'Evaluation'.
Part 2:	Introduction and Unit 6: Material from *Groups* 2/5, 'Making sense of data' (written by the compiler).
Unit 7:	Material from *Organisations and Communities* 3/4, 'Surveys' (written by the compiler).
Unit 8:	Material from *Groups* 2/4. 'Interviewing' (written by the compiler with additional material from an earlier assignment briefing).

Zoo activity in Unit 10 reprinted from *Zoo Animal Management* Vol. 1, page 44, written by Stan Everiss and published by NEC.

All other quotations are acknowledged in the text and listed in the References section of Bell (1993) or of the course itself (p. 117).

Growing up researching: a note by the compiler

As I say in the Introduction, this course is based on a book on research methods by Judith Bell. If you read the acknowledgements page of her book *Doing Your Research Project*, you will see that the advice and information in the book is itself based on the research experience of quite a number of people. First and foremost, of course, is Judith Bell herself, but she also mentions friends, Open University colleagues, and students, including those on an OU course, EP851, which contained earlier versions of some chapters from the book.

The experience of all these 'expert practitioners' is naturally also available to you as a student on this course. I have had the benefit as well, as compiler, of thorough, helpful and extremely positive comments from Judith Bell herself – for which I am most grateful.

However, this course reflects the experience of still more researchers, some expert, and some beginners: my own academic colleagues and students, including those at the YMCA National College in London, with whom I have worked over the years. And of course it inevitably reflects my own experience – some of it painful – of doing research of various kinds over a period of twenty-five years or so. By sharing these experiences, I hope to help you avoid some of the pitfalls that I (and others) have tumbled into in the past.

My first real piece of research was very nearly a total disaster. I decided to do a senior thesis as part of my final year's work at an American university. In theory it should have been easy: I chose a topic for which all the primary source materials were available on microfilm at the University library, in a series of early American printed books and pamphlets. I had a hypothesis about what I might find, and had only to work through this treasure trove and find evidence which would confirm or reject my hypothesis. In practice, it took far longer than I had anticipated, and there was a nightmare last-minute dash to complete, including a whole night spent in the library surrounded by microfilms. Even so, I ended up handing it in late and feeling rather disappointed with the result of all my hard work.

When I came to do research for my DPhil, I knew I would have to be more disciplined, especially as I was working while I studied. I asked fellow students and colleagues what they would have done differently if they had had their research to do over again, and they all said 'Start writing up your research from Day 1.' This was extremely good advice, and you will find it repeated throughout this course. Fortunately there were seminars at which I could 'try out' draft chapters of my thesis, and I had a supervisor who asked for written drafts rather than verbal reports, so I managed my time rather better than before. The only snag was that I had chosen a topic which required a reading knowledge of Greek and Latin – but I met my future husband in the Greek evening class, so even that proved to have its benefits.

Since then I have had to investigate and write up various pieces of research in connection with my work. Some recent examples, all for different clients, include:

- a study of a computer-based training course for retail trainees, which involved observing and interviewing trainees and their tutors, and working my way through the course as a 'pretend trainee'
- writing up a piece of action research on the training needs of youth workers helping young people with special learning difficulties
- a history of the National Extension College
- currently, a small-scale study, using questionnaires, which aims to help a major distance-learning provider collect evaluations of its courses from students.

Each of these projects required different methods, and a different approach; once again, I hope that these varied experiences will be of benefit to you through your study of this course.

When I began doing research as an undergraduate, no one suggested that there were skills and techniques of research which could be learned: you just got on with it. If I had had the benefit of a course like this, I like to think that I would have done a better first job, and I am certain that the experience would have been much less painful. I hope it works for you; if so, even that night spent in the library will begin to seem worthwhile.

With very best wishes,

Linda Deer Richardson

Contents (Course plan)

Introduction

Techniques of Investigation is a course based on the book *Doing Your Research Project* by Judith Bell (1993, 2nd edition). You will need a copy of this book as part of your materials for the course. It also includes some material from a distance-learning course, using the same book, which was prepared by Judith Bell and others for the Distance Learning Programme of the University of Sheffield's Division of Education. Both of these were designed for students undertaking educational research, and for that reason many of the examples are taken from the field of education. However, the basic principles of research are the same in any field, and I hope that *Techniques of Investigation* will be useful to you, whatever the topic of your research.

As Judith Bell points out in her introduction to *Doing Your Research Project*, the problems of doing research are also much the same whether you are producing a small project report or a PhD thesis. Whatever the size of your investigation, you will need to:

- select a topic
- identify the objectives of your study
- plan and design a suitable methodology
- devise appropriate research instruments
- negotiate access to institutions, materials and people
- collect, analyse and present the information

and finally

- produce a report or dissertation.

The list may sound daunting, but the course is designed to guide you through this process, and help you to develop the skills and techniques you will need, step by step. It takes you from the initial stage of selecting a topic, right through to the stage of producing your final report or dissertation.

| Reading | Before we go on to look at the course itself, stop and read the Introduction to *Doing Your Research Project* (which I shall refer to as Bell from now on). You will find it on pages 1–2 of the book. Notice the aims that Judith Bell sets out for the book, and also the definition she gives of 'research'. |

About the course

The reading you have just done will have introduced you to the set book for the course. But you may still have some questions about the course itself. In the rest of this Introduction, we look at:

1 who the course is for
2 how the course works
3 course features.

Who is the course for?

The short answer is 'anyone who wants, or needs, to do a piece of research and write it up'. Throughout the course, we assume that you will be conducting your own investigation as you work through the units. As Judith Bell says in her

Introduction, the best, indeed the only, way to learn how to do research is by doing it. You may be working on your own or with the help of a tutor.

The sort of investigation you do, and your reasons for doing research, will vary, of course, depending on your own circumstances. You may be studying for a degree, diploma or professional qualification which includes a piece of research as part of the coursework. You may need to conduct an investigation as part of your job, or even be employed as a researcher. Or you may be keen on researching some topic for its own sake, or to find something out: perhaps investigating a piece of local history, or surveying facilities available in your community, as part of a campaign for improvement. If you are a student, you may have been given a topic to investigate; if not, you may still have a clear idea already of what you need or want to investigate.

If, however, you don't have a research project in mind, I suggest ways of choosing a topic that interests you, and that could form the basis of a useful piece of research. If you prefer, you can choose one of the topics listed at the end of Unit 2, and follow up this topic as you work through the course. This will help you to develop the skills you will need for conducting an investigation in the future, but even if you are doing the course just to develop your skills as a researcher, you will get more out of it if you can choose a topic that interests you and means something to you personally.

The examples of projects given by Bell relate particularly to research which has to be completed in two or three months – what she calls '100-hour projects'. But you should find the course equally useful if your project has a shorter or longer timescale, and also if you are conducting research for a higher degree, particularly in the social sciences and humanities. If you are studying for a research degree within a college, polytechnic or university, you will of course have a supervisor to help you with your investigation. Supervisors are busy people, however, and your time with your supervisor may be limited. If you can use this course to become familiar with basic approaches and techniques, and to apply them to your own research topic, you will be able to make full use of your time with your supervisor for priority issues related to your subject.

How does the course work?

The course is divided into three main parts, as shown on the Contents (Course plan) pages.

I will assume that at the start of the course you will probably have a general idea of the area you need or want to investigate, but that you probably will not have 'firmed up' your research plan or thought very much about how to go about your investigation.

Part 1 of the course, 'Planning', therefore aims to help you to select a final topic, identify the questions you want to ask, do some initial library research, and choose appropriate research methods. At the end of Part 1 you should have a detailed outline and schedule worked out for your research, and have a broad idea of what has been written on your subject by other people, and what you will need to do to complete your investigation.

Part 2, 'Collecting Data', guides you through the process of collecting data from written sources, and from people, using a variety of different research instruments or methods. You are unlikely to need to use all of them in your investigation, but we suggest you read through all the units in this part to get an overview, and then work carefully through the one(s) which apply to your own study. At the end of Part 2, you will have developed research tools for collecting the data you need, and sorted out any 'glitches' in your research methods.

Part 3, 'Analysing and Presenting your Data', assumes that you have begun to use your research tools to gather data, and offers guidance on analysing the information you collect and writing up the final report. One important piece of advice is to analyse and write up as you go, rather than leaving it all to the end!

What features does the course have?

There are 12 units in the course, each of which covers a different stage of the research process. The work for each unit includes reading from the corresponding chapter of the Bell set book, and working through the appropriate stage of your own investigation. It is difficult to estimate how long each unit will take you, since it will depend upon the size and complexity of your research project and also on how much time you have to do the work. But as you work through Part 1, you will be asked to draw up a timescale or schedule for your project, taking account of what needs to be done and the time you have available. This should give you a clearer idea of the time you will need to spend on each unit.

At the beginning of each part of the course, you will find an Introduction which outlines what it will be covering. At the beginning of each unit, there is also a list of the topics covered in that unit, which you can use to check that you have covered everything, or when using the course for reference.

As you go through each unit, you will be asked to read sections from the corresponding chapter of the set book, Bell. There will usually be some suggestions on how to approach this – e.g. whether to skim, read carefully and take notes, or apply the reading to your own situation.

In each unit you will also find activities. Like the readings, these are identified by a heading in the left margin and printed in a different typeface. This is a signal for you to stop and think, and maybe jot down some notes based on your own experience. You should have a notebook ready to hand for these jottings. Activities are there to give you a chance to try out new techniques, and get to grips with the actual details of planning and conducting research. Often there is some comment or feedback following these activity sections. These comments are not 'right answers' and you should not worry if your ideas are different from the ones I put forward. The important thing is to stop and think, or try out a new skill. Remember that you learn to do research by doing it!

If you are working through the course with a tutor (provided by your college, your firm or NEC) you will also have someone to advise you on methods and approaches. You should contact your tutor any time you feel 'stuck' or in need of advice, and you will also be asked to send work to him or her at intervals throughout the course. The course has five assignments, three in Part 1 and one each at the ends of Part 2 and Part 3. These are regular opportunities for you to check out with your tutor how the project is going, and seek guidance and advice if necessary. In general, assignments are based on work you will need to do anyway to complete your project, rather than asking you to do 'extra' work. Of course you can still do the work for the assignments even if you are working without a tutor.

At the ends of some units, you will find one or more books or articles under the heading 'Suggested reading'. As this is a practical course, and as you will probably have quite enough reading to do related to your topic, I have only included books or articles that I feel will be especially useful to some aspect of your research. *None of them are essential.*

Full references to sources mentioned in the course text which are not in Bell are also listed at the end of the course (p. 117). The form of reference I use in the text is the Harvard system, which is mentioned in Unit 4: briefly, 'Borg (1963:188)' refers you to the work listed by Borg that was published in 1963, page 188.

Investigating a topic that interests you can (and should) be an exciting experience – we hope that this course will help you to get the most from it.

Good luck with your investigation!

PART I: PLANNING

Introduction

In Part 1, we take you from your initial vague thoughts about choosing a topic to a detailed blueprint of what you hope to achieve. At the end of this part of the course, you should have:

- chosen a topic for your investigation

- decided on the central questions you plan to investigate

- prepared an outline

- worked out how long your research should take

- learned an effective way of keeping records of your findings

- done the basic reading on your topic

- chosen a research strategy

- thought about how to gain access to the information you need

- drawn up a code of practice if your research involves people.

All of this comes into the general category of planning, or laying the groundwork, for your study. You may be eager to get on with your research – I hope you are – and you may wonder whether spending time on all this planning is really worthwhile. Let me assure you that it is. Of course, you can't predict in advance exactly what you will find out, and there certainly will be things that you don't expect, however carefully you plan: otherwise, there would be little point in doing the research in the first place! But if you plan your investigation from the beginning, you will be able to make the most of the time you have available, and minimise the frustration which seems an inevitable part of any piece of research.

12

Unit 1: Choosing your tools

1   **Why do research?**

2   **Basic types of research**

3   **Six approaches to research**

4   **Which method for you?**

5   **Checklist**

6   **Suggested reading**

In this first unit, we shall:

* look at your reasons for doing research, and your initial ideas for a topic
* list several different types or styles of research, and the methods associated with each, to help you select an approach that will be appropriate to the topic you have in mind.

1 Why do research?

Even if you don't have a topic clear in your mind as yet, you must have had *some* reason for enrolling on this course! Use the activity below to record your thoughts on why you have chosen to do a piece of research.

Activity 1

What are the reasons you have for wanting to embark on a piece of research, or to investigate some topic? Jot them down.

If you are doing your investigation as part of a course of study, your reasons for doing it will presumably include 'completing the course' or 'getting my qualification'. Hopefully you will also choose a topic which interests you, and which you want to find out more about. You may also have some practical benefits in view.

If you are not a student, however, your reasons for investigating may be even more varied: you may have chosen to investigate some topic simply because you are interested in learning more about it, or to record what is known about it. Historical investigations are often of this descriptive type.

Or you may be interested in promoting some kind of action as a result of your investigation: a change in the way your organisation does things, an increase in funding, an opportunity to find out what is really happening, or what people really want, so that you or the organisation for which you are doing the investigation can plan accordingly. So the reasons you gave may have included any of the following, or others:

* learning
* management, planning, taking decisions
* policy change. ⏐

What purpose, what audience, what action?

Another way of looking at this question is to say that, whatever you investigate, you should be clear about:

- what it is for: its **purpose**
- who it is for: its **audience**
- what you expect to happen as a result: the **action**.

Even if you have not chosen a topic, you should be able to answer these questions about the piece of work you plan to do.

<table>
<tr><td>Activity 2</td><td>Your investigation – jot down what is:

1 its purpose?
2 its audience?
3 the action you expect as a result of doing it?</td></tr>
</table>

You should be able to get a clue as to its purpose from your answers to Activity 1. But if you are finding this exercise difficult, the easiest bit is probably 'audience'. Ask yourself:

- Who will read the report of my investigation once it is completed?

Then you should be able to get at 'purpose' and 'action' by asking:

- Why am I doing this report for this particular audience?
  and
- What do I expect my readers to know or do as a result of reading my report?

What do you want to investigate?

So far, we have not spoken about the actual topic of your investigation. We will come back to this in Unit 2, but before we go on to look at the different types of investigation, take a few minutes to note down your ideas so far. You may at this stage have a very clear idea of your chosen topic, or it may be very vague, with lots of possible options. Never mind – at this stage, all I want you to do is to write down a brief note of your ideas. You might find it easiest to try and answer the question 'What do I want to find out as the result of my investigation?' This will give you a focus for the rest of the unit, in which we look at a number of different ways of approaching a research project, and ask you to think about which ones might be suitable for what you have in mind.

<table>
<tr><td>Activity 3</td><td>What do you hope to find out in your investigation? Make a brief note of your ideas for a topic, or the main questions you hope to answer. If you have ideas about particular methods you hope to use, jot those down too.</td></tr>
</table>

2 Basic types of research

In this section of the unit, we look at some ways of dividing investigations into several broad types or categories, according to the **scope** of the research and the basic **methodology** used. In the next section, we will consider the main features of six important **styles** of research. The idea is to give you an overview of possible ways of tackling a research project, so that you can begin to think about which approach might suit you best.

Broad or narrow scope?

One way of distinguishing between approaches to a topic is to compare their **scope**. 'Scope' refers to the quantity of events or actions or circumstances to be considered in the investigation. It can be broad or narrow, according to how much or how little material is included.

Basically, a broad-scope piece of research covers a broader area, but is able to tackle it in less depth. An example might be a survey, with hundreds or even thousands of respondents, while an example of a narrow-scope approach might be a case study of an individual or small group.

Both approaches have their advantages and disadvantages, as the table below illustrates:

Narrow scope	Broad scope
More certainty about the conclusions	Less certainty about the conclusions
More definite guide to future action	Less definite guide to future action
Less general applicability	More general applicability

A good analogy is with photography: narrow scope corresponds to close-up, where you get much detail but a small subject, while broad scope is like the long shot where you get a wide picture but not much detail.

Which approach seems more likely to suit the topic you have in mind for your investigation?

Qualitative or quantitative methodology?

Another way of distinguishing between research projects is by their use of **quantitative** or **qualitative** approaches. Many pieces of research will include both, but we can still identify important differences in the assumptions of researchers using one approach or the other.

Reading

Judith Bell describes the main features of quantitative and qualitative research in the Introduction to Chapter 1, 'Approaches to Educational Research' (pages 5–6). Read pages 5–6 now, and note down:

- the differences between these two groups of researchers
- which seem more likely to you to use broad-scope methods, and which narrow-scope
- any advantages or disadvantages you can see for either approach.

As Bell says, quantitative researchers are interested in facts and their relationships, and in details that can be measured to produce generalisable results.

Qualitative researchers tend to be sceptical of the use of 'scientific' methods, such as statistical analysis, for the study of human beings. They tend to focus on individuals and their perceptions of the world.

Quantitative research often makes use of statistical analysis: in this case it needs to be broad in scope if the results are to be statistically valid.

Qualitative research tends to be narrow in scope: its focus is the individual case study, or the small group.

Once again, each approach has its advantages and disadvantages.

Quantitative research is generally considered more precise, and hence more reliable. But the information it gives you needs to be carefully evaluated for meaning.

Qualitative research data is more difficult to collect, and to interpret. However, it can give a more rounded picture of its subject, by taking note of features that quantitative research tends to ignore.

<table>
<tr><td>

Activity 4

</td><td>

Which of these research topics do you think would benefit from a quantitative (counting) approach, and which from a qualitative (observing, comparing) one?

If you choose quantitative, what would you, as researcher, need to 'count'?

Would the research in each case be broad or narrow in scope?

(Work out your own answers before looking ahead at my thoughts on this.)

Topics:
1. A study of voter opinions on a particular candidate.
2. An investigation of the lifestyle in a small, isolated village.
3. A report on differences in child-rearing practices among parents in a playgroup.
4. An attempt to find out the preference of cats for a certain cat food.

</td></tr>
</table>

1. This question would almost certainly be dealt with using quantitative methods, such as a voter survey or opinion poll. What you would actually be counting is the number of people who answered each question in a particular way – 'Yes', 'No' or 'Don't Know', for instance. It would need to be broad in scope if the results were to be statistically useful.

2. 'Lifestyle' is the sort of thing which market researchers claim to be able to measure using quantitative methods, but I think the researcher here would probably be interested in aspects of life in the village which could not be counted, and might use observation or interviews to gather data. Compared with 1, it would be narrow in scope.

3. This could be approached using either quantitative methods, such as a questionnaire or structured interview, or qualitative ones like observing and recording the behaviour of parents with their children. The researcher might decide to use a mixture of quantitative and qualitative methods, in fact. It would be a narrow-scope study, because it deals with a small group of people.

4. This could be a piece of quantitative research, in the form of an experiment which measured how many cats chose a particular food under certain conditions. The scope would depend on the number of cats available, but the number of subjects could be quite small.

3 Six approaches to research

As Bell points out, you don't need a detailed knowledge of the various approaches to research in order to plan and carry out an investigation. However, a brief look at some major research styles will give you some idea of the different ways you could go about planning your research project. It will also help you understand some of the technical terms, or 'jargon', that you may meet in reports of research by other people.

The six styles or approaches we shall be introducing are:

- action research
- the case study
- the ethnographic style
- the survey
- the experimental style
- historical or 'documents' research.

Reading

Read carefully through the descriptions of the first five of these approaches in Chapter 1 of Bell, pages 6–13.

As you read about each approach, ask yourself whether it seems suitable for the type of investigation you have in mind. You might like to take notes, using the grid in Activity 5 below as a model.

Historical or 'documents' research

What about historical research? Bell does not mention this type of research in Chapter 1, but this is also an important approach, and one which might interest you. Borg (1963:188) describes historical research as:

the systematic and objective location, evaluation, and syntheses of evidence in order to establish facts and draw conclusions concerning past events.

The procedures involved in planning, gathering and evaluating data are much the same as for any other type of research, but as Borg says,

perhaps the major difference between historical research and other forms of scientific research is that historical research must deal with data that are already in existence. (1963:190)

It is not only historical research which involves the analysis of documentary evidence. Extracting evidence from documents such as minutes of meetings or reports is often a necessary component of any research. On the face of it, this is a straightforward enough task. However, before you begin any study of documents, it is important to understand the nature of documentary evidence.

Reading

Skim Chapter 6 in Bell, 'The Analysis of Documentary Evidence', looking for the main features of this method of research, its differences from the other methods and whether it looks useful to you.

We will come back to this chapter in Bell, and you will find guidelines for research using written sources and other documentary evidence in Units 3, 4 and 6 below.

Activity 5

As you read about the six approaches in Bell, you might like to list the main characteristics of each approach on the grid printed on the next page. This will give you a useful checklist for later reference, and you can add to it as you read further and find out more.

Approach	Special features/ characteristics	Methods associated with this approach	Any likely problems for you?
Action research			
Case study			
Ethnographic style			
Surveys			
Experimental style			
Historical research			

You can compare your notes on the main features and associated methods of each approach with mine in the checklist at the end of this unit.

If you want more detail on these approaches, you will find some useful sources listed in the 'Suggested reading' list at the end of the unit.

4 Which method for you?

The approach you take, and the methods you choose, will depend on what you want to find out, and the resources you have available.

<u>Activity 6</u>

Look back at your answers to Activity 3 (your initial thoughts on your topic) and your notes on the chart summarising the six approaches described above (Activity 5).

Are there likely to be any problems for you as an individual researcher in adopting any of the approaches?

Would it be possible to overcome these problems if you were carrying out a project in your own institution or an institution known to you?

Consider the timescale for your research project. Would one or more of the approaches require more time than is available? It may be that some approaches demand more statistical knowledge than you have at present, or would take too long to complete satisfactorily. If so, that does not necessarily mean that the methods associated with that approach have to be abandoned.

Make a note of the approaches which seem likely to be suitable for your investigation, and also of any which seem unsuitable for any reason.

As will be clear from your reading, no approach requires or automatically rejects any particular method of investigation. You will need to select methods of collecting information which are appropriate for the task: in fact, you can only make a final choice of approach and methods when you are quite clear what information you need. We will continue this process of deciding on the right tools for the job in Units 2 and 3. However, your reading for this unit will have helped to give you some ideas about the characteristics of certain styles of research. When you begin to plan your project, you will be in a position to decide which, if any, of the approaches discussed in this unit are likely to be right for your investigation.

Here is a final activity to help you think about matching appropriate tools to different kinds of investigation.

| Activity 7 | Choose an appropriate research style or approach, from the six discussed above, for each of the following topics: |

1   A study of students' opinions of the grant system in the UK.

2   A piece of research to measure the effect of two different techniques of memorisation on short-term memory.

3   A report on the lives of members of a street gang in an urban neighbourhood.

4   Research into the causes of communication difficulties in a department where you work, with the aim of improving communication.

5   A study of the families who have lived in a nineteenth-century terrace since it was built.

6   A report on how a local campaign against a new road was planned and carried out.

When you have finished, you can compare your ideas with mine below.

1   This looks like a suitable subject for a survey, using either questionnaires or structured interviews to gather information from a group of students chosen to be representative.

2   This is the sort of topic which could be tackled by experimental methods, using matched groups of subjects, half of which used each of the methods being compared.

3   This is a classic subject for an ethnographic approach, in which the researcher would take part in the life of the gang over a period of time, and attempt to understand their way of life 'from the inside'.

4   The practical aim of this research suggests the action research approach.

5   Because of its historical nature, this study would need to be based on documents, such as census reports and parish registers.

6   A topic like this could be treated as a case study, which might shed light on the reasons why one campaign succeeded while others perhaps failed.

Checklist

Choosing your tools: six approaches to research

Action research

Features:	participant researching in own institution
	purpose is action: change of policy etc.: identifying and solving problems
	on the spot/ongoing
	most likely on the job
Methods:	observation, questionnaires, diaries, interviews, case studies
Problems:	researcher is insider.

Case study

Features:	narrow scope, limited scale
Methods:	observation, interviews
	may lead into or follow up survey
Problems:	selection; personal approach: can another person relate to what you have done?

Ethnographic style

Features:	researcher becomes participant in society
Method:	observation, descriptive recording
Problems:	time, taking on approach of group; acceptance; generalisability.

Experimental style

Features:	deals with things you can measure
Methods:	matched groups, pretest, control for single variable.
Problems:	large scale; difficult and expensive to run.

Surveys

Features:	aims to draw out information which can be compared, analysed
	usually relatively broad-scale; quantitative; facts not relationships
Methods:	self-complete questionnaires, interviewer with questionnaires, checklists, schedules
Problems:	representative sample; design of questions; only certain kinds of information: what, where, when, how but not why?

Historical research

Features:	uses documents rather than face-to-face collecting methods.
	can be broad or narrow in scope: doable at a distance
Methods:	selection and analysis of documents, literature
Problems:	analysing and interpreting evidence.

6 Suggested reading

There are two works which stand out as being helpful on basic methods of research: Louis Cohen and Lawrence Manion's *Research Methods in Education* (Cohen and Manion 1989) – this is the latest edition of a classic text on research methods. It covers a wide range of research methods, including surveys, experimental methods, action research, historical research, case study and others. Some of them are likely to be beyond the resources of the individual researcher with a limited timescale, but if you need to investigate a particular research method in more detail, this is a useful source with lots of examples.

Patrick McNeill's *Research Methods* (McNeill 1990) – designed primarily for sociology students, this is an approachable introduction to social science methods including surveys, experiment, ethnographic approaches and the use of secondary data such as statistics.

22

Unit 2: Planning your investigation

1 Making plans

Some of us are planners by nature: whether it is a holiday or a piece of work, some people seem to enjoy making careful and even elaborate plans, and are happiest when they feel that everything is foreseen and under control.

Others (and I would probably place myself in this category) prefer to take things as they come, and are constantly 'tilting the deadline' as a result.

Whether you are a 'natural planner' or not, a research project is a major piece of work, and you will need to do some planning before you start if you are to avoid wasting time and effort. That is what this unit is about. By the end of the unit, you should have:

- drawn up a shortlist of topics that interest you
- chosen a likely topic and written to your tutor to explain your choice
- drawn up a preliminary list of questions to focus your thinking
- firmed up your objectives, and decided whether you need a hypothesis
- drawn up an initial outline
- done some exploratory reading
- worked out a draft timescale.

When you have done all this, you will be in an excellent position to move on to the next stage, and actually begin your research. Don't skimp this planning stage in your eagerness to 'get on': it is important to lay the foundations, and your first and second assignment will ask you to check out your plan with your tutor.

Activity 1

Stop and think for a moment about the kinds of things you do when planning something, whether it is a piece of work, a shopping trip, a holiday or any other activity. Jot them down.

When I thought about planning a shopping trip – perhaps the mad dash into London which is usually all I have time for before Christmas – I realised that I had to think about several things. For instance:

1   What do I *really* need to accomplish? What is important, and what can be left if necessary?

2   In what order should I do things: where should I go first?

My way of tackling this is usually to compile a list of present ideas, and a list of the shops I plan to visit, starting with the best prospects and taking note of their location to avoid backtracking.

3   How much time (and money!) do I have available?

Planning a research project is no different from planning a holiday, or a shopping trip – only it is more complex, and so needs more careful planning. You still need to think about:

- what your priorities are
- what needs to be done, and in what order
- what resources you have available.

2 Choosing a topic

As I said in the Introduction, we assume that, at this stage of the course, you will have a general idea of an area you need or want to investigate, but that you will probably not have a detailed research plan and may not have thought very much about how to go about your investigation.

If you are a student, you may have been given a topic to research, but in many cases the decision will be up to you. If your plan is to investigate some aspect of your work situation, you may be free to choose your topic, or it may be determined by what others in your organisation think needs investigating. If you are doing the course out of interest, you will be free to choose a topic that interests you. The assignments for this course are all based on your investigation of your own topic, but if you are doing the course simply to learn about research methods and really cannot come up with a topic of your own, you will find some suggestions at the end of this unit (page 26). You might like to look at them now to see the sort of investigation that you might do on a fairly limited timescale, but before you choose, try to think whether there are any aspects of your own situation – your workplace, your neighbourhood, an organisation you belong to – that you have questions about, which an investigation could shed some light on.

Activity 2

What topics interest you? Write down *all* the ideas you have for topics which you feel would be sufficiently interesting for you to spend time investigating them. You don't need to be precise at this stage: concentrate on getting your ideas down.

If you are interested in investigating a topic in education, for instance, you might consider something like one of the following:

- the introduction of a significant curriculum change
- a study of the role of a head of department or a subject head
- the management of resources in a school or college
- the appraisal of teachers
- an investigation into in-service education and training of teachers in your institution or area
- a survey of the use of accommodation and/or equipment.

Your topic doesn't have to be practical, but you might find it most interesting to choose something which is of direct relevance to you – say to your work. Try to identify aspects of your work which interest you and which you consider would be worth investigating – and start from there.

Explore your ideas

Once you have a list of possible topics, you need to do some work to decide which one to select.

Read the first section of Chapter 2 in Bell, 'Planning the Project', on 'Selecting a Topic' (pages 15–17). Make a note of the things she suggests you do before going on – and do them!

So before you take a final decision on your topic, you should:

1   Discuss possible topics with colleagues at work, or fellow students. Ask for their views about the feasibility of your ideas. If you are likely to need the cooperation of colleagues or others (for instance, as subjects for interviews or surveys), sound them out now. Ask whether, for example, permission would be given for you to observe in meetings, see confidential documents, distribute questionnaires or arrange interviews. Never assume 'it will be all right'. It might not be. There may be some regulation which prohibits data collection without official permission.

2   Consult your library's catalogues, and the librarian, about the amount of literature available in each of your possible subject areas. But remember that at this stage you are not carrying out a major literature search. You are simply aiming to give yourself a general idea of the amount of work done by others on topics that interest you: so confine yourself to a superficial glance at what is readily available.

3   Discuss your ideas with your supervisor, if you have one. Assignment 1, below gives you a chance to discuss your shortlist of topics with your 'Techniques of Investigation' tutor.

Select a tentative topic

As your discussions and reading proceed, you will begin to refine your thoughts. The next step is to decide which of your proposed topics you think will be possible in the time available, and likely to produce useful results.

Before you make your final decision, you have an opportunity to discuss alternatives with your tutor.

Write a letter to your tutor introducing yourself. Explain why you are taking the course, and what you hope to gain from it. Describe the topic you have tentatively chosen, or the topics you are considering, and say why you think they would be worthwhile for you to investigate. If you have decided to use one of the topic suggestions at the end of the unit, say which one you have chosen and why it interests you.

Based on the work you did in Unit 1, say what approach and methods you think would work best for your topic, and why.

Finally, if you have any questions about any aspect of your study, add them to your letter.

3 Focusing your topic

Once you have had comments back from your tutor, you can make a final choice of topic. Next, you will need to begin to draw up a list of aspects of the topic you intend to investigate, and identify questions to which you will need to find answers.

Your 'first thoughts' list of questions

Remember that you can't do everything, and try to identify which aspects of the topic really interest you. A good way is to start with questions for which you would like to find answers.

Write down questions as you think of them; don't worry at this stage about the wording or the order in which they belong. You will inevitably think of more as your investigation proceeds, but here is an activity to get you started.

1   Write down as many questions as you can think of which you hope your investigation will help you to answer. Take five or ten minutes on this.

2   Go through your list. For each question, ask yourself:

'What will I need to do to find an answer to this question?'

'How useful will the information be to the overall topic?'

3   Cross out any questions that you can't work out how to find answers to, or that don't seem useful.

4   For each remaining question, write down one thing you will need to do to get an answer.

5   What methods could you use?

Suppose, for instance, that you have decided to investigate barriers to learning among mature undergraduates. Your 'first thoughts' list might look something like the one on page 17 of Bell.

Reading

Read the section in Bell on 'The "First Thoughts" List and Establishing the Focus of the Study' (pages 17–18).

Activity 5

Take another look at the 'first thoughts' list you did for Activity 4. Are there any terms which are unclear, or likely to be unclear to other people? Try to work out what you really mean. Can you identify the aims and objectives of your study? If so, write them down. They may well change, but be as precise as you can.

Do you need a hypothesis?

Some research projects begin with a hypothesis, which can be defined as a tentative statement of what you think you are likely to find out in your investigation. The investigation itself then seeks to prove or disprove the hypothesis. For instance, in the example above about the role of the school governors, a possible hypothesis would be that governors do (or do not) play a major role in curriculum decisions.

Whether your investigation needs a hypothesis or not might depend in part on the kind of study it is.

Reading

Read the section 'Hypothesis or Objectives?' from Chapter 2 in Bell (pages 18–19). Is the type of study you have in mind likely to need a hypothesis, or will objectives be enough?

As Bell points out, what is really important is not whether your study has a hypothesis, but whether you are clear in your mind about what you plan to investigate and how you plan to go about it. Inevitably, your plans will change in detail as you work through your research. But unless you have a clear plan, you will not be able to decide on appropriate methods for your study, and you may end up in the position of the unfortunate researchers Bell mentions, with 'a huge quantity of data and little idea of what to do with it'.

Prepare an outline

Let's assume that you have chosen a topic you want to investigate, drawn up a list of questions you want to answer and tried to clarify them, and come up with a hypothesis if you think your study will benefit from one.

The next stage is to prepare an outline, which brings the information you have gathered so far together.

Unit 2   26   Techniques of Investigation

At this stage, a typical outline might include:

- Proposed title for your study
- Aim or hypothesis – what you hope to achieve
- Main questions you hope to answer
- Possible methods of investigation – what you will need to do in order to answer your questions
- Initial list of written sources to consult.

This outline will form part of Assignment 2, which you will find at the end of this unit.

Before you try to draw up an outline for the topic you have chosen, take a look at the sample outline Bell provides, for the project on mature undergraduates which we looked at earlier.

Activity 6

Look at the suggestions on pages 20 and 21 of Chapter 2 in Bell, and then produce your own preliminary outline, either on similar lines or in a format which seems most useful to you.

What will you need to ask and to find out? List those questions. Then consider which are the best or most likely ways of obtaining the information you need, and list those under 'Possible methods of investigation'.

4 Planning your reading

To complete your outline, you will need to go back to the library.

Activity 7

Go back to the library and draw up a short list of possible sources for your final choice of topic, building on the work you did early in the unit when you checked out the sources available for the range of topics that interested you. You cannot read everything that has been written on your topic in the time you are likely to have available for your project, so try to get an idea of the references which are most frequently mentioned in the literature. These may be key works, and the fact that they are frequently quoted by other authors is often a good indication that what they have to say is worth reading. If some of the works referred to are not available in your main library or have to be ordered, you may have to eliminate them from your list of possible sources on grounds of time and cost.

Add the books and articles that look most useful to your draft outline: you don't need to read them thoroughly at this stage, only identify your most important sources.

5 Planning your time

The final, important stage of your initial plan is to plan your time, taking account of what needs to be done and the time you have available.

Reading

Read the section on 'Timing' in Chapter 2 in Bell (pages 21–22). Take particular notice of Bell's advice on what to do if things do not go as you plan: the golden rule is not to be afraid to ask for help.

Like the project outline, your schedule may need to be adjusted, but it is important to start out with an idea of how long the different stages are likely to take, especially if you are working to a deadline set by your employer or educational institution.

Activity 8

Look back at your list of things you will need to do, or methods of investigation, which should be part of your draft outline (Activity 6). How long will each one take? Can you foresee any problems, e.g. meetings are infrequent, you need to arrange access?

Draw up a list to show when you expect to complete the following stages, working back from the due date of your research report if there is one:

- finish collecting data
- finish analysis/begin writing
- complete writing.

6 Checklist

Check that you have completed all the stages in the 'Planning the Project Checklist' on pages 22–23 in Bell before going on to complete Assignment 2.

Assignment 2

Send your tutor:

1 your 'first thoughts' list in its revised form (Activities 4, 5)

2 your preliminary outline, including the initial list of literature to be consulted (Activities 6, 7)

3 your timetable or list of 'key dates' (Activity 8)

4 a note of any questions or problems you have at this stage.

Suggested topics for research

I have already said that, if you are free to choose your own research topic, it is much better if you can identify a question that interests you: something you really want to find out about. But if you are doing the course mainly to get practice in research methods, and you really cannot think of a suitable topic, here are some suggestions that you can use to focus your research, or adapt to suit your own situation and interests. I have tried to choose suggestions which will give you a choice of approaches and research methods as well.

1 How do local people feel about some service or amenity that is provided for them, or a recent change in their situation? Can you do some independent investigation to find out how justified their praise or complaints seem to be?

Some possibilities:
- commuters and British Rail
- council or private tenants and housing conditions, repairs, rents etc.
- shoppers and local shopping facilities
- parents and local schooling or play facilities
- young people and local facilities for leisure or recreation.

2 As an alternative, how would a particular group in your community like to change some aspect of their situation? You may be able to investigate a local campaign or pressure group and find out what they would like to change and why, what sort of people are involved and how the campaign or group came about.

Other possibilities:
- What changes in design would people dwelling in a modern block of flats like to see in the block where they live?
- What solutions can residents living near a busy road, a noisy factory or some other nuisance suggest for improving their situation?

3   Choose a group or organisation that is unfamiliar and try to identify how they see themselves, what their assumptions and beliefs about themselves and other people are, and how they live on a daily basis. You might choose members of a different religious or ethnic group, people much younger or older than yourself, people working in a very different type of organisation than your own or even in a different department within the same organisation.

4   Is there some aspect of the situation where you work – client or customer satisfaction, training needs, the impact of new technology, or anything else that you can identify – that would be worth investigating as a piece of action research?

5   What changes have taken place to your house, the neighbourhood where you live, an organisation you belong to or work for, over the past 30, 50, 100 years?

Unit 3: Sharpening your tools

At this stage in the course, you should have chosen a topic, identified key questions you want to try to answer and prepared an outline, including an initial list of books and articles to be consulted.

Before you continue with your research, you should wait for a response from your tutor to the outline and questions you sent him or her for Assignment 2, at the end of the last unit. But in the meantime, this unit is a chance to see whether your basic research tools – keeping records and making notes – are in good sharp working order.

If you are a beginner at doing research, you may be well aware that you are not quite sure of the best way to go about keeping notes of what you have read and what you find out.

On the other hand, if you are a student or an experienced worker, manager or teacher, for instance, you may think that you already know all you need to about keeping records of your reading and your research. You may indeed have already established a method that does the job and suits you very well. But are you really sure that you have nothing more to learn?

I mentioned at the beginning that this course allows you to benefit from the experience of a large number of researchers, both experts and beginners, who have contributed to the information in the set book and in the course itself. In this unit, I shall therefore try to bring together my own experience of recording research findings with that of these other contributors. However confident of your own methods you may feel, you may decide that perhaps you could learn something from methods which have been used successfully by many researchers before you. If so, read on.

1 Capturing your data

Computer users talk about 'data capture'. It is a term which somehow suggests that information is like a wild animal, and needs to be stalked and brought back alive. The image is not a bad one: information can sometimes be difficult to track down, and it can be very frustrating if after all your hard work the essential detail or reference vanishes just when you need it. On page 24, Bell describes an experience that is all too familiar to most researchers:

Finding information in the first place can be hard enough. Finding it again some time afterwards can be even harder unless your methods of recording and filing are thorough and systematic. We all think we shall remember, but after several weeks of reading, analysing and selecting, memory becomes faulty. After a few months, we may vaguely recall having read something some time about the topic being studied, but when and where escapes us. After a longer period, the chances of remembering are remote.

Because information is so slippery, you need to get in the habit of recording everything that you read – even if it turns out to be a 'dead end' in the long run. Whatever method you choose, the sooner you start using a systematic system of record-keeping, the more chance you will have of holding on to the information you collect.

There are a number of different methods of keeping records and making notes. This unit describes one of the most popular ways of doing this – using file cards.

2 Playing your cards

One very popular method of keeping a record of your reading is by using file cards. That is the method I shall be describing in this unit, not because it is the only way of recording your findings, but because it is simple, flexible and useful in various ways – to keep a note of references for your bibliography, to note themes and topics which may become chapters or sections in your report, to keep track of quotations, and so on. You may have used a method like this, and found it useful. Or you may be saying 'But why bother with all this business of special cards? I keep notes on scraps of paper, or the backs of old envelopes, and I can always find what I'm looking for.'

Activity 1

You may be a member yourself of the back-of-an-old-envelope school of recording, but can you think of any possible advantages of a more systematic system, based on cards (or sheets of paper of uniform size)?

Jot down your thoughts before you go on to read what Bell has to say about this.

Reading

Read the introduction to Chapter 3 in Bell (pages 24–25) now, and also the sections headed 'The Card Index' and 'Referencing' (pages 25–28).

I would imagine that every researcher has had the experience of having to track down books or journal articles a second time because he or she forgot to note some part of the reference the first time around. (It certainly added days to the time needed to complete my own DPhil thesis, despite my best efforts!) But if you get in the habit *now* of noting the basic information about everything you read for your project on individual cards, you can save yourself the frustrating backtracking that Bell describes.

The list of essential information half-way down page 26 in Bell is what you will need for your references: more about these later in the unit. But, as Bell points out, you may need additional information as well, depending on whether you plan to buy the book, look for it in your local library or order it by inter-library loan.

Your initial information about sources is likely to come from a bibliography like the British National Bibliography (BNB) or a library catalogue. (We will be looking at the question of how you go about gathering this information in the next unit.) Page 44 in Bell gives an example, taken from the BNB. But how much of this information should you include on your record card, apart from the information needed for your references? The sample card on page 27 gives hints on this. Let's try another example to be sure you have the idea.

<hr />

Activity 2

Look at the reproduction below of an entry from the BNB Index Volume 1, 1980. How much of this information do you think it would be important to record for future reference? You might like to write it in on the blank card below.

> 372.1'2'0120926 — Primary schools. Head-teachers.
> **Leadership.** *United States. Case*
> *studies*
> **Jentz, Barry C.** Leadership and learning :
> personal change in a professional setting / [by]
> Barry C. Jentz and Joan W. Wofford. — New
> York ; London [etc.] : McGraw-Hill, 1979. —
> xv,181,[1]p ; 24cm.
> ISBN 0-07-032497-2 : £6.10
>
> (B80-01592)

Think about what information you would need:

- for your references
- to locate the book in a library
- to purchase the book.

How would you set out this information, so that it was clear to read? Try this for yourself before looking at my sample card below.

Here is the way I filled in the card:

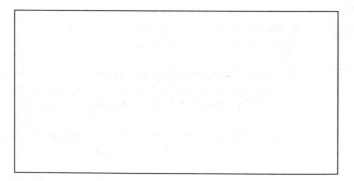

You may not need all of this information, depending on your purpose in making the record. You will obviously need the author(s), title, publisher, place of publication and date of publication for your bibliography or references, as

<hr />

mentioned on page 26 of Bell. I included an abbreviated form of the Dewey decimal number (the most common form of library classification system) from the top left corner of the BNB entry. This might be enough to help me find the book on the shelf in my own library, but I would probably be wiser to wait and add that information to the card when I came to look up the book in the catalogue of my particular library, since classification systems do vary. You might need to know where you found this reference, in case you need to consult it again, so I have included a note on this in brackets at the bottom of the card. (The year, 1980, is included in the number in the bottom right corner of the BNB entry.) The price would only be useful if you (or the library) wanted to buy a copy of the book, and the ISBN (International Standard Book Number) would again be useful for this purpose, or for ordering the book from another library by inter-library loan. You probably did not feel you needed to include details like the number of pages or the size of the book. However, you might have decided to include the search terms (or subject categories) from the beginning of the entry, to help you locate other books on the same subject, or perhaps a note that this was a book of case studies, neither of which I included on my card.

As this example illustrates, one important use of cards is to keep track of the details about each book or article that you will need when preparing your bibliography or references.

Keeping track of references

You have already met some of the rules for referencing: you will be aware of what information you will need to include in your bibliography or references, and what you should do about abbreviations. (If you have forgotten, look again at page 26 of Bell.)

However, you might also know that there are several different methods of referencing that you could use, assuming of course that your institution does not have a standard format which you are asked to follow.

If you have a choice, it makes sense to use a system which suits your needs, and is simple to use. In Chapter 3, Bell describes one of several common referencing methods, the **Harvard system**.

Reading

Read Bell's description of referencing methods, in the section 'Referencing' (pages 26–28). Notice the tips she gives for remembering how to set out the information you need for book and article references.

You might like to prepare your own model cards, using the examples in Figure 4.2 in Bell (pages 27 and 28) as a guide.

In the course on research methods that she wrote for the University of Sheffield, Bell reports that many research students she knows have adopted this method of preparing model cards to remind them of the format for references, and say it makes recording very easy: for one thing, it is easy to check that you are being consistent about things like underlining, quote marks and punctuation. Some students prefer to set out their cards in exactly the way they want the list of references or bibliography to appear, like this:

LYONS G (1981) Teacher Careers and Career Perceptions. Windsor, NFER-Nelson.

They say that this leaves more space on the card for other information and makes the format for references clearer when cards are handed over to the typist.

If you are using a computer with word processor to prepare your project report, you may feel that all this talk of file cards is ancient technology. You may prefer to use a database program on your computer to record your references, and to shuffle them into alphabetical order or whatever order you like. But unless you are able to take your computer to the library, and balance it on the top of the card catalogue as you search, you are likely to find cards, or some similar method, useful even so as a method of initial 'data capture'.

Recording quotations

Another useful way of using your card file system is to keep a note of quotations you might want to use in your report.

Reading

Bell discusses this on pages 30–31 of Chapter 3, in the section headed 'Noting Quotations', and I suggest you have a look at this now.

As she says, photocopies (if available) are probably the easiest way of recording quotations that you think you may want to use, but you may still find cards useful for keeping a note of their source. Remember that you will need to include page numbers when referencing quotations – another advantage of photocopies, as you will usually be able to read the page number on the copy. This is another one of those niggling details that can send you back to the library at the end of your project, so if photocopies aren't an option, try to check that you make a note of the pages as you go, perhaps on your cards.

It's worth taking extra care checking that you copy quotations exactly as written, into your notes and into the final report, using three dots (...) to mark any omissions. You would be surprised how often quotations are inaccurate – it's very easy to write down what you *think* someone said or wrote, rather than what is actually on record.

3 Using your notes to structure and sequence your report

So far we have been looking at specific uses of recording: to make a note of sources consulted in our reading, so that we have the information available for referencing, quotation or locating these sources again.

It's also possible to use record cards, or sheets of paper, as a means of structuring and sequencing your findings. Cards or sheets can be used to set up subject classifications which can be used to group the information you gather into categories, and perhaps suggest new linkings or additional topics. These categories can be merged, divided, or put in a different order as you gather new evidence or your ideas change. And when you come to write up your report, you will have a skeleton or outline, and probably your table of contents as well.

Bell discusses this aspect of recording beginning on page 29, and I suggest you look at this now.

Reading

Read the sections on note-taking and categorising evidence in Bell (pages 29–30), and take a note of any ideas that look useful to you.

Once again, if you are using computerised methods of gathering and writing up your research, such as a database program, you should already have available the flexibility and ease of sorting which Bell suggests that cards can provide the researcher. The principles are the same, however, whether you use cards, sheets of paper, or some electronic method of grouping and sorting your data.

Take a few minutes to think about possible subject headings or categories for your chosen topic, using the examples in Bell as a guide. Jot them down on index cards or sheets of paper which you can then use to arrange your notes or cards into sections according to subject.

There are also short cuts you can use to save time and make your data-capture methods even more effective. One example is the use of **source keys**.

If you will be using particular sources frequently in your research, you can use a source key to speed up your recording of information. Instead of writing the title, author and so on, all you need to write in your notes is the source key or reference number – though of course you will need to have another set of notes or cards somewhere with the full reference keyed to the number.

Whether you use notes on cards or on sheets of paper, there is one more advantage to a flexible system of recording when it comes to thinking about your topic. You will remember that Bell suggests you write the subject key in pencil, so that categories can be altered as your ideas change. Particularly in the early stages of your project, it may be a mistake to make your topics or categories too rigid, and cards or separate sheets can help you arrange and rearrange your materials as it suits you. C. Wright Mills, in the Appendix to *The Sociological Imagination* (1959) in which he describes his own research methods, recommends rearranging your file as a good way to stimulate your imagination, and help you to think about your topic in new ways. Dropping a full box of index cards on the floor is a research disaster to be dreaded, but perhaps it has its positive side!

Activity 4

Before you go on to the next unit, look out your own reference cards or notes of the reading you have done so far, and compare them with the examples on pages 27 and 28 in Bell, and the Checklist on pages 31–32 there.

Take a good look at your notes, especially your references to books and articles you have read. Are they in a consistent format? Are any essential items of information missing? Think about the method of recording you intend to adopt in your research. Will you adopt any of the suggestions given in this unit? If so, which?

4 The rewards of virtue

When taking notes of our sources, we are all inclined to miss out minor details such as the date of publication or the name of the publisher. These may seem unimportant at the time. But if your notes are not complete, you can find yourself having to spend days or even weeks going back to libraries to check missing references or other bits of information.

The message of this unit is that this frustrating process can be avoided, if you are willing to take a little care from the beginning of your research.

Reading

Bell describes the rewards of good recording habits on page 31 in the section headed 'A Lot of Fuss about Nothing?' Have a look at this now, to finish off your work for the unit and encourage you for what lies ahead!

5 Checklist

Finally, look again at the 'Keeping Records and Making Notes Checklist' on pages 31–32 in Bell. Are you following the guidelines in the checklist? If not – why not?

It may sound fiddly, especially if (like me) you are not the organised type but prefer the 'old envelopes' approach to recording. But following these simple rules can make your research path much, much smoother – believe me!

Unit 4: Getting an overview

1   Why do a literature review?

2   Establishing a framework

3   Conducting the search

4   Writing up

5   Checklist

6   Suggested reading

In this unit, we look at the beginning stages of your research proper – reviewing the literature. You have already begun to do this in your preliminary reading for Assignment 2, but you now need to think about doing a more thorough survey and preparing a more detailed account of what other people have written which is relevant to your chosen topic.

This survey or overview of the field, which is usually written up as an introduction to your project report, is known as a literature review.

1 Why do a literature review?

The simple answer to the question 'Why do a literature review?' may be 'because it is required'. Most academic research projects require a review of the literature relating to the topic being investigated. The bigger the project, the more comprehensive this review will need to be. An extensive study of the literature, and a critical review of what has been written on your topic by other people, will be required for a PhD thesis. Smaller projects will not require anything so extensive, but will still expect you to show an understanding of the state of knowledge in your chosen field.

Activity 1

Apart from the fact that it may well be a requirement of the piece of work you are engaged in, can you think of any other reasons why it might be useful to read as much as time allows about other work done in the area of your project topic, *before* starting your own investigation?

Note down your thoughts before going on.

Reading

Now read the introduction to Chapter 4 in Bell, 'Reviewing the Literature', and the next section, headed 'Analytical and Theoretical Frameworks' (pages 33–34). Compare your reasons with what Bell has to say here.

As Bell reveals, a literature review is a vital tool for getting an *overview* of your chosen topic – that's why it is important to do it early on in your research. It can help you to:

- put your research into the context of work which has been done by others – and avoid duplication of effort

- gain insight into ways of collecting and analysing data and presenting your findings

- check your hypothesis or objectives for completeness and accuracy

- begin to order and classify your data, and develop a structure for your report.

Remember that it isn't enough simply to collect a mass of facts. You need to order and classify your data into a pattern, based on a theory or model, which makes sense and explains how the facts fit together.

A literature review can help you to structure your ideas and build up a pattern of explanation. As you read what others have written about your topic area, you may get ideas about how you could organize your own research, and you will also get a feel for the kinds of questions people are asking and the answers they accept, which may help you develop your own thesis or argument.

2 Establishing a framework

The literature review, then, should establish the framework for your research, both for you as researcher and for the reader. It should provide the reader with a picture of the state of knowledge and of major questions in the subject area being investigated. It needs to be more than a list of 'what I have read': ideally, as Haywood and Wragg (1982:2) point out, it should 'show that the writer has studied existing work in the field with insight'.

This is not easy. Haywood and Wragg complain that so-called 'critical reviews' of the literature are more likely to be what they call 'uncritical reviews':

the furniture sale catalogue, in which everything merits a one-paragraph entry no matter how skilfully it has been conducted: Bloggs (1975) found this, Smith (1976) found that, Jones (1977) found the other, Bloggs, Smith and Jones (1978) found happiness in heaven.

(Haywood and Wragg 1982:2: quoted in Bell, page 35)

Activity 2

Read the section in Bell headed 'The Critical Review of the Literature' (pages 35–38). Pay particular attention to the literature review by Alan Woodley reproduced on pages 35–38.

This is the introduction to a study entitled 'Taking Account of Mature Students', produced by a researcher with the Open University in 1985. You may well be unfamiliar with Woodley's field of study, but you should still be able to decide whether or not this is a successful review.

Ask yourself the following questions (suggested by Bell on page 35 and make up your mind whether Woodley has successfully introduced his topic and placed his own research in the context of work by others.

Does his introduction put you in the picture?

Does it give you some idea of the work that has been done already, and prepare you for what is to follow?

Does it suggest that he 'has studied existing work in the field with insight'?

I think that Alan Woodley has done a good job in this review. He has given us an overall picture of his field, and the place of his research within it. He does this by discussing what has been done by other researchers and explaining how his own research will build on what has been done already.

Notice that he does not get bogged down in too much detail. He has not tried to provide an account of everything he has read, along the lines of the 'furniture sale catalogue' satirised by Haywood and Wragg. Instead, it appears that he has had the discipline to leave out many of the books and articles he read because they were not directly relevant to his own research. All of this suggests to me that he has indeed 'studied existing work in the field with insight'.

You can if you wish use Woodley's review as a kind of model, when you come to write your own literature review.

Activity 3

You might like to begin by noting down what seem to you the 'rules for writing a good literature review' which Woodley's work illustrates.

Here are my notes – yours will no doubt be different, but what is important is that you will have identified the features which made the review successful for you.

1   First of all, the review suggests that you need to read enough to get an overall picture of your topic area. This will allow you to place your own planned study in context, just as Woodley has done.

2   What you write should also provide an overview of your topic, which will guide both you and the reader. You can think of it as a kind of story, to which your research will add another chapter. What Woodley did was to:

   • discuss in general terms what had been done by other researchers. Notice that he begins by *stating the question* that they were all attempting to answer ('Do mature students do better or worse than younger students?') and *compares* the different studies as he goes along.

   • explain how his study would fit into this overall pattern ('The aim of the present study was to extend Walker's work to all British universities, so that these and other relationships could be tested out on a much larger sample ...').

3   Remember that not everything you read will be worth a place in your review. Make sure that everything you include is relevant, and forms part of the 'story' you are trying to tell.

Identifying possible headings

As we said at the beginning of the unit, reading a selection of the relevant literature at the beginning of your research can help you to begin to sort out 'the wood from the trees'. You can begin to identify which are the important subjects, headings or topics for your research, and how they might fit together.

You may remember that the reading for Unit 3 suggested that you should put subject or topic headings, in pencil, on your note cards to make it easier to group them together for analysis. But where do these headings come from?

One possible answer is that your initial reading may help you to identify possible subtopics and headings which can be used to structure your report. There is a delicate balance here. I warned in Unit 2 that it isn't a good idea simply to gather piles of data without some idea of what you are trying to find out – for one thing, you would find it impossible to know what to select, and you can't select everything! But on the other hand, if you try to identify topics or headings before doing any exploratory work, you are likely to build up false categories which will need to be abandoned as you gain knowledge from your reading and fact-finding.

What is likely to happen in practice is something like this. As you read, categories or groupings will occur to you, and you can note them down. As you collect your data, you may be able to classify information into the categories you have already identified, but you will also identify new categories. So as your research proceeds, you will need to build on and amend your original structure, while you keep looking for ways in which you can organise your facts into a coherent pattern which allows you to compare and contrast, to explain the relationships among facts, and possibly to move towards the formulation of a theory.

In an ideal world, this would be made easier because you would have finished all the reading before you started to think about collecting your own data. Certainly you should do as much reading on the topic as you can early on, for all the reasons which we discussed at the beginning of this unit. But it may not be possible to obtain copies of the books or articles you need precisely when you want them. Do the best you can, but keep an eye on your schedule: you may need to start collecting other data before the reading is finished, especially if you need to work around the dates of meetings, term dates or other factors outside your control.

3 Conducting the search

How, then, should you go about the task of identifying what you need to read?

If you are a student, part of the work may have been done for you. If you have been given a topic to investigate, then you will probably also have been given lists of books and articles to read as well. This will give you a starting point, and in a small project it may provide all the sources you need. Your supervisor will probably also have suggestions, and may be willing to guide you to the most important references. In this case, your only search problems will be finding the books and articles on your list – and, if you are lucky, they will be in your institution or department's own library.

But if you have chosen your own topic, you will first need to find out what has been published in your field, and then track your sources down in libraries and other collections. The work you did for Assignment 2 is a beginning, and will have given you some idea of what is available. Your time is likely to be limited, and you will inevitably only be able to read a selection of the relevant books, articles and reviews. So how do you choose?

As Bell explains, for you it is especially important:

1   to find the most relevant published materials quickly

2   to avoid getting bogged down or sidetracked in your search

3   to get into the habit of recording information from your reading so that it can be easily found and understood weeks, months or even years later.

We talked about Point 3 in the last unit; this unit, and particularly this section of the unit, is about how to find the materials you need quickly, and without getting bogged down in what my old biology lecturer used to call 'the entangling details'.

Access to libraries

You may think that you know all about how to use libraries, but how much do you really know about what is available in the libraries near you, and how they can help you in your research?

Reading

Read the sections in Bell headed 'Locating Published Materials' and 'Access to Libraries' down to the heading 'What Are You Looking For?' (pages 38–40). These describe the different kinds of libraries, and give a general view of the services available.

Activity 4

As Bell says, the first step is to find your library. Ask yourself:

•   Which library (or libraries) do you plan to use for your research?

•   What type of library is it – a public library or an academic library?

•   Are there other libraries in the area which you might be able to use? Even if you are not a student or a teacher, it is worth asking for permission to visit an academic library if it has materials you need for your research.

If you are pursuing some form of documents research, you may also need to investigate other sources of written records, such as archives and record offices – but that is for later on. For the moment your concern is what other people have written on your topic, and for that a library is what you need.

If you are not familiar with your chosen library and its facilities, an initial visit is a good idea. Find out:

- what type of classification system it uses (most public libraries and many college libraries use the Dewey system, but some specialist academic libraries have systems of their own) and where books on your topic are likely to be located

- what sort of material is available in other forms: microfilm or microfiche, for instance

- what sorts of indices and bibliographies are available to help you in your search.

If you can't find what you are looking for – ask! My own experience is that librarians are extremely willing to help, and may astound you with their detailed knowledge of the collection. They are the experts, after all.

If you are using the library of the institution where you are a student (or a lecturer or teacher), you will presumably already be familiar with what it has to offer and how the holdings are arranged. Even so, there may be other academic or even public libraries in your area which could be useful to your research.

Spend some time identifying which library has most to offer you, arranging access if necessary, and making an initial visit if you are not familiar with what the library has to offer.

Defining your search criteria

This is a fancy way of saying 'What *exactly* are you looking for?'

To use any library, particularly a major research library, without getting sidetracked by the wealth of material available, you need to be very clear about the answer to this question. As Bell points out, large academic libraries can seem like Aladdin's caves, full of dazzling treasures. But such treasure troves can be dangerous – it is easy to get lost, and to waste valuable time. The way to avoid this is to define what you are looking for as carefully as possible – and then be firm about excluding materials that don't fit your search pattern.

Reading

In the next section of Chapter 4 Bell takes you through the process of defining your search terms, using as an example the topic of mature undergraduates. Read from the heading 'What Are You Looking For?' (page 40) and follow through the first four stages of the outline on 'Planning a Literature Search' on pages 41 and 42 .

Activity 5

Before you go on, use the outline below to work through the first four stages of the search process for your own topic, and make sure that you are clear on the **topic**, the **terminology** and the **parameters** of your search. In alphabetical order, list as many alternative **search terms** as you can think of.

Defining your search criteria:

1   Select the topic.

2   Define the terminology. (Are you clear what you mean? Are there alternative terms?)

3   Define parameters:

 • Language?

 • Geography? (UK sources only, or are there reasons for reading more widely?)

 • Time period?

 • Type of material?

 • Sector?

4   List possible search terms.

Locating references to books and journal articles

Once you have defined the terms of your search as precisely as you can, it should be safe to go back to the library and try to locate books and articles relevant to your topic. The first step is to consult reference sources, like library catalogues, bibliographies and indices, to see what is available. Bell deals with this phase of the literature search, again using the example of mature undergraduates, on pages 42–49.

Reading

Read to the end of the section, following through the remaining stages of the literature search outline. You might like to take notes of the main points as you go, to guide your own research. Notice that Bell's examples of reference sources focus on those which are particularly relevant to educational research. Similar bibliographies and indices exist for other research areas – ask the librarian if you need help.

I have summarised the main points about the bibliographical sources Bell mentions below.

Library catalogues

Library catalogues may be in the form of cards or microfiches, or on computer. (Some major academic libraries, including the British Library, still have their main catalogues in bound volumes.) There are likely to be separate author, title and classified catalogues, but the place to start is with the **subject catalogue** if there is one.

Use your search terms and note down all the relevant library **class numbers** for your topic.

Use the **classified catalogue** (for libraries using the Dewey system) to find out which books on your topic the library holds. (The classified catalogue will also group books by subject, using the Dewey classifications.)

Repeat the process as you identify new search terms.

Check the **author** or **title catalogue** at the end of your search, to locate additional references you found in bibliographies or indices.

Bibliographies

For books:

British National Bibliography (BNB)

- There are annual volumes since 1950; listings are cumulative.
- Check the **index** for each year to locate additional search terms.
- Search the **subject catalogue** under the headings you have identified, to locate references.
- Full bibliographical details are given in the **classified sequence**.

For journals:

For example, for educational research, the *British Education Index (BEI)*

- This has been published since 1954, with annual cumulative volumes.
- Use your search terms to check the subject list.

Similar indices to periodicals are available in other subject areas: ask the librarian for guidance.

Apart from library catalogues, bibliographies and indices, there are other sources available to help in your search:

Abstracts

These provide summaries of books, articles, etc. Bell lists major sources in the field of education.

Similar lists are available for other subjects. Check *Ulrich's International Periodicals Directory*.

Theses

Subject listings are, for example, on microfiche in *British Education Theses Index 1950–1980 (BETI)*. Bell lists other sources on page 49. Order theses by inter-library loan if you need to and have time.

Computer searches

- You can use library facilities or your own microcomputer linked to a computerised database.
- These require careful search strategy, and can be expensive.

(See 'Suggested Reading' below, if you want to know more about this method.)

Activity 6

Use the reference sources available in your chosen library (or libraries) to locate references to books and articles which meet your search criteria. This is the point at which careful recording of bibliographical details, following the guidelines we introduced in Unit 3, will start to pay off. Keep a careful record of the references you collect, using cards or another method that suits you.

Finding the materials

Having collected as much information as you have time for about what sources are available, it's time to get them off the shelves and have a look at them.

Reading

Read the final section of Chapter 4 in Bell, 'Obtaining the Materials' (page 50).

The advice Bell gives on checking out your sources to see whether they are likely to be worth spending time on is valuable, and can save you a lot of time (and possibly inter-library loan fees).

To summarise her advice:

- For books: check the preface, the chapter headings and chapter summaries if they exist.
- For journals: use the abstract to check out the content of the article.
- Look at the publication date: is the information likely to be dated?
- What does information from bibliographies, indices or other books and articles tell you about the work?

Knowing when to stop

Once you have started on your literature search, the next problem is to decide when you have done enough reading for your project. Once again, Bell gives useful advice on this (on page 50) and it is worth looking back at this now.

Remember that you will never have time to read everything you could read. The general rule is that you should read enough to get a general feel for the field in which you will be doing your research – enough to identify major issues, and the main contributors on whose work you will be building. If you are a student, or otherwise working to a deadline, it may be time which determines how much reading you are able to do. You need to keep your final hand-in date in mind, and adjust your schedule as you go along if necessary. Ask your supervisor, your employer or your tutor for advice if you need it.

4 Writing up

Activity 7

When you have completed your preliminary reading, write a draft review of the literature, following the model of Alan Woodley's review in Activity 2. Yours will almost certainly not be as long or as detailed as his: the main point is to make clear what each source you mention contributes to the question you plan to investigate, rather than producing a mere list or 'furniture sale catalogue'.

Don't worry if at this stage your review is imperfect or incomplete: the important thing is to get something down while the reading is still fresh in your mind, and the connections between the different books or articles are clear. Remember the basic rule that writing the report begins as soon as you have any information to hand, not at the end of the project!

Your draft review will form part of the work for Assignment 3, at the end of Part 1 of the course.

5 Checklist

Before you go on to Unit 5, review the work for this unit by consulting the 'Reviewing the Literature Checklist' on page 51 in Bell, and check that you are following her guidelines.

6 Suggested reading

As ever, it's much more useful to actually conduct a literature search for yourself than to read about how to do it. Dale and Carty (1985) and Haywood and Wragg (1982) provide useful guides. If you are interested in the possibility of using a computer search to collect references and abstracts, you might like to consult Ray Hammond's *The On-line Handbook* (1984). Some of the information in this edition is now outdated, but it is still a good place to start if you are new to computer communications.

Unit 5: Mapping a research strategy

1 **Choosing your methods**

2 **Arranging access**

3 **A code of practice**

4 **Checklist** Assignment 3

5 **Project progress check: end of Part 1**

By this stage in the course, you should have:

- selected a provisional title for your project
- agreed your project outline and tentative schedule of work with your 'Techniques of Investigation' tutor
- identified questions to be investigated
- carried out an initial literature search.

By now you should have quite a good general idea of where you want to go, and some ideas about how to get there.

This is the last unit in Part 1 of the course. It is about mapping your journey.

By the end of Unit 5, you should have:

- chosen your method(s) of research
- planned access to information and people
- thought about the issue of confidentiality.

Assignment 3, at the end of this unit (and of Part 1) will help you to check that your plan is in good shape before you start the main part of your research.

1 Choosing your methods

By now you should have a general idea of the best way of obtaining answers to the questions you have identified. Your investigation may be based entirely on library research, but it is more likely that you will need to use other methods of investigation, involving people.

In determining which methods you will be able to use, you will need to keep two things in mind:

1   the demands of your topic
2   the resources available to you.

What methods does the topic need?

I suggest we start with an activity to show how you might begin to work out what methods a particular topic 'needs'.

<table>
<tr><td>Activity 1</td><td>

1   Choose one topic from the list below.

2   Write down at least two *questions* which the topic suggests to you.

3   For each question, write down at least one *task*, i.e. one thing you would need to do or find out in order to get an answer to the question.

4   For each *task*, suggest an appropriate *method*. (Look back at Unit 1 if you need to remind yourself of the different approaches and methods we introduced there.)

</td></tr>
</table>

Topics:

1   The involvement of the governors/management committee in the work of a school, club or community centre.

2   The attitude of older people to the presence of a club/centre/project for children or young people in their neighbourhood.

3   Recreational needs of young people in a neighbourhood.

Now do the same thing for your chosen research topic.

<table>
<tr><td>Activity 2</td><td>

Take the list of questions you hope to answer in your research, and the proposed methods of investigation as you identified them in your outline. (This should by now have been revised, following comments from your tutor on Assignment 2.)

For each question on your list, write down how you could go about finding the answer – that is:

1   Write down the things you will need to do or find out in order to get an answer to the question.

2   For each thing to do, suggest a method you could use. At this stage, your notes may be very brief, e.g. 'read books'; 'ask local residents'. Try to identify the actual tasks which will have to be done by you or someone else.

3   Look back at Activities 5 and 6 in Unit 1, where you compared possible research approaches and methods using a chart, and identified ones that seemed appropriate to your topic area. Have your ideas changed?

4   Go through your notes of possible methods for each question (Point 2 above) and weed out any that seem unrealistic. On a separate sheet, list all the research methods you plan to use in your study.

</td></tr>
</table>

Among the methods you may have mentioned are:

•   getting information from books and journals ('library research')

•   questionnaires

•   interviews

- diaries or recordings made by yourself or others
- observation. ⌐

We will be looking at these methods in more detail in Part 2 of the course. You might like to look ahead at the units in Part 2 which discuss your chosen method(s) to get a clearer idea of the sort of work each will involve.

What are your resources?

We said earlier that the methods you choose will depend on two factors:

1 the demands of the topic
2 the resources available to you.

<table>
<tr><td>Activity 3</td><td>Jot down the resources you will have available for your research project.</td></tr>
</table>

One resource you will probably have mentioned, which is likely to be in short supply, is time! Most research projects have a due date, and the timetable you drew up for Assignment 1 had to take note of the time you will have available to do the research.

Here is an opportunity to check out your earlier estimate, now that you have a clearer notion of what work your project will involve.

<table>
<tr><td>Activity 4</td><td>Go through your list of questions again, and the methods you have chosen for answering them (Activity 2).</td></tr>
</table>

- Try to work out how much time you will need to complete the tasks you have identified.
- You may find that it helps to divide your work into stages, like those on the chart below.
- Use the chart to estimate how much time each stage of your research will take.
- Cross out any stages or tasks that you have completed, or that don't apply to you.
- Write the number of hours/days you estimate each task will need.
- What is your total? Are you being realistic?

Stages of research	Time allowed
I *Planning and preparation* Define topic/scope of research Carry out draft review of literature Choose methods Choose sample group Decide how results will be analysed	
II *The pilot study* Produce research instrument (e.g. questionnaire, interview schedule) Refine details of the study Pilot research instrument	
III *Research* Gather data	
IV *Analysis of the results* Analyse data	
V *Writing* Write report	
VI *Action* Disseminate/use the research	

2 Arranging access

In Activity 2, I asked you to note down 'the actual tasks which will have to be done by you or someone else'. Unless your project is entirely based on research using books and other documents, it will probably involve other people. Even if your research is entirely based on written documents, you may have to negotiate access with the holders of those documents.

Who are the people you need to consult?

Activity 5

Look back at your list of research methods for Activity 2 and mark any which involve other people.

Who are these people, and what will you need to do in order to gain the information you need from them? Make some notes.

What permissions do you need?

It may be necessary for you to seek formal permission for your research: for instance, from your employer or from someone in authority in the institution you plan to investigate. It makes sense to take the appropriate steps to negotiate access early on in your research. Bell explains how to go about it.

Reading

Read the first section of Chapter 5 in Bell, 'Negotiating Access and the Problems of "Inside" Research', stopping when you come to the paragraph about Stephen Waters (we will come back to him later).

How can you make people more willing to help you?

This question may sound manipulative, but it is worth thinking carefully about how to approach the individuals or organisations who will need to give permission for your research, or whose cooperation you need if it is to be successful. Partly, this is good manners; and it also involves trying to see your project as it will appear to other people.

Daphne Johnson (1984) points out that the need to arrange access is the same whether research is being done in person or by a postal questionnaire. She summarises the tasks involved as follows:

1   imparting the conviction that the investigation is a worthwhile piece of work and the investigator a competent person to carry it out

2   explaining why the investigation seeks the cooperation of the person or institution being approached

3   indicating the use to be made of the research material.

She points out that negotiation of research access is unlikely to be a once-and-for-all process: information and assurances may need to be given to a succession of audiences in a variety of ways. As we have seen, research in a school, for instance, may mean gaining the approval of education officers in the authority, the head teacher and teachers and pupils from whom information is sought. You might like to think about the different techniques needed to explain what you are doing to these different audiences. And Johnson warns that:

whatever the research method being used ... agreement to research access must be kept in good repair throughout the enquiry. ... If files are left in disarray, papers borrowed and not returned, or respondents subjected to too lengthy or frequent interviews, at inconvenient times, the researcher's welcome will be worn out.

(Johnson 1984: 11)

Ask yourself: why *should* your sources cooperate? What can you do to help make it seem worth their while?

<table>
<tr><td>Activity 6</td><td>

Make a note of:

- the people or institutions with whom you will need to negotiate access for your investigation
- what you plan to say to them, keeping in mind Daphne Johnson's three tasks outlined above.
</td></tr>
</table>

3 A code of practice

In any investigation which involves other people as informants, there are likely to be sensitive areas. You will need to keep this in mind when deciding the questions you want to ask, and we will come back to this in Part 2 when we look at the design of questionnaires and interviews.

The questions you will probably need to keep in mind when planning access are:

- Will informants need the protection of anonymity or confidentiality?
- What do informants need to know about the results of your investigation?
- Will there be limits on what you can report?

What do you mean by anonymity and confidentiality?

You will need to work out guidelines for your own investigation.

If you promise confidentiality, you will need to decide what that means. If it means that individuals will not be named, will the individuals concerned be identifiable anyway? Does it mean that only you and your tutor will see the report? What exactly does it mean?

The question of anonymity is not as straightforward as it might seem. For example, if you are investigating in a school, and there is only one head of History, everyone who knows the school will know who is meant in your report by 'the head of History' and the fact that you do not name the person will not make any difference to this. Anonymity to outsiders is one thing; anonymity within the organisation is likely to be something else again. The guiding rule, as Adelman, Jenkins and Kemmis (1977:146–147) suggest, is that you should remember that *other people* will have to live with the consequences of your reporting.

Simons (1979), writing about the evaluation of policy in an educational institution, further develops this theme of anonymity and confidentiality. She makes the point that the principle of confidentiality is just as problematic in a school where the researcher is a member of staff as it is for outsiders. She draws attention to the difficulties faced by staff members of a school or college who are conducting research in their own institution, and reminds us that comments made during a 'chat in the staff room over a cup of tea' or informally outside of school should be regarded as confidential. It would be breaking faith to make use of such comments, unless the people concerned give permission for them to be quoted. If you are researching in your own institution, maintaining good relations during and after the research is important and colleagues should not be damaged or made vulnerable by your actions.

What information do your sources need?

Another aspect of this code of practice is the question of giving your informants access to your research, either in draft form for comment or once it has been completed.

Some researchers suggest that informants should have the right to comment or to edit the researcher's accounts of their views and actions. On the face of it, this makes sense and is a courtesy to which informants should be entitled. However, there are problems for a researcher working to a restricted timescale. In an audio tape prepared for the Open University course EP851, 'Applied Studies in Educational Management', Daphne Johnson recalls one occasion when the head of a school had made repeated changes to draft texts of an interview so that the research was seriously delayed. The question then arises as to whether he was making corrections on matters of fact, or whether he wished to change what he actually said. An individual researcher should be careful not to promise what cannot be delivered and it may be that for this project you will not have time to check back with each person you interview.

| Activity 7 | Look at the guidelines below, used by a researcher conducting research in the school where he was a teacher. |

1   All participants will be offered the opportunity to remain anonymous.

2   All information will be treated with the strictest confidentiality.

3   Interviewees will have the opportunity to verify statements when the research is in draft form.

4   Participants will receive a copy of the final report.

5   The research is to be assessed by the Open University for examination purposes only, but should the question of publication arise at a later date, permission will be sought from the participants.

6   The research will attempt to explore educational management in practice. It is hoped the final report may be of benefit to the school and to those who take part.

What seem to you to be the good points about these guidelines – keeping in mind Daphne Johnson's advice, and the comments about confidentiality we quoted above?

Are there any of the guidelines that you think might cause difficulties in practice, however? Which ones, and why?

What tactics could you use to reduce any problems you identify?

| Reading | The researcher in this case was Stephen Waters, who was conducting research in his own school as part of his work for an Open University advanced diploma in educational management. |

You can read an account of the way in which he went about negotiating access, and the difficulties he encountered, on pages 53–54 in Bell. His own comments on the problems which his research guidelines (quoted above) caused him in practice are on pages 54–57 in Bell. You might like to compare them with your answers to Activity 7.

What can you not report?

Related to these questions is the question of whether, because of confidentiality, there will be limits on what you can report. Here is an Activity which may suggest some of the possible problem areas.

<table>
<tr><td>

Activity 8
</td><td>

Suppose you were investigating:

- the attitude of pupils in a school to authority
- the behaviour of a 'deviant' group such as drug users
- the day-to-day behaviour within a community where you live.

Choose one of these examples and work out what guidelines you would need on:

- confidentiality/anonymity
- arranging access and offering information to informants
- limiting the information you include in your report.

As already mentioned, the golden rule is that other people will have to deal with the consequences of your reporting, and you need to keep that in mind throughout your investigation.
</td></tr>
<tr><td>

Activity 9
</td><td>

Refer back to your project outline, which should by now have been agreed with your tutor, and to the list of people who will be asked to help in your research (Activity 5). Decide how you will deal with the problems of anonymity and confidentiality. Discuss these issues with colleagues who are likely to be participants in your research, and with other key people (your principal, headteacher, head of department, etc.) Now draw up your conditions and guarantees for the conduct of the research. Once this is done, you will need to make copies of the guarantees and of the project outline to hand to participants. Everyone will then be fully in the picture about your plans, and there will be no misunderstandings later.
</td></tr>
</table>

4 Checklist

Read Bell's conclusion to Chapter 5 (bottom of page 57 to page 58) and use the 'Negotiating Access Checklist' on pages 58–59 to make certain that you have covered all aspects of clearing the way for your research.

Then go on to Assignment 3 below. You should find that you have done the work for it already, but now is your chance to catch up if you have fallen behind.

<table>
<tr><td>

Assignment 3
</td><td>

Send your tutor:

- your draft review of the literature (Unit 4 work)
- a note on your choice of method(s) and why you have selected them
- your draft guidelines on confidentiality (Activity 9), if appropriate
- your plan for access to documents and people and a more detailed timetable (Activities 4–6).
</td></tr>
</table>

5 Project progress check: end of Part 1

Before you go on to Part 2, check that you have:

- chosen a provisional title for your project

- agreed your project outline with your tutor (including any amendments)

- identified questions to be investigated, and defined the objectives of your study or formulated a hypothesis

- agreed with your tutor the best ways of obtaining the information you need in order to answer these questions and achieve your objectives

- prepared a schedule of work, and revised it if necessary

- started a card index system and produced model cards, or devised a system of recording which is consistent

- carried out an initial literature search and produced a draft literature review (which may be incomplete at this stage)

- carried out the necessary procedures to gain access to documents, institutions and people.

Your schedule will remind you of how much time you have before the project report needs to be completed. Different stages of your research will inevitably overlap to some extent: for instance, you may not have completed all the reading you hope to do, and if you are planning to use methods such as interviews, questionnaires or observation studies, they will have to fit in with the commitments of your subjects. But if at any stage you find you are getting seriously behind schedule, contact your tutor and agree on ways in which you can adjust your original plans.

There is never enough time to do everything!

PART 2:   COLLECTING DATA

Introduction

This part of the course takes you through the stages of doing research proper: choosing an appropriate methodology and collecting data in a systematic way which will allow you to analyse your findings.

You have already made a start at selecting appropriate methods in Part 1, but in Part 2 you will have an opportunity to examine a range of possible research methods in much more depth, and learn how to design and test research instruments for each.

Remember that (as Bell warns) the first question you need to be clear on is not 'Which methodology shall I use?' but 'What do I need to know and why?' As a result of your work in Part 1, you should by now have chosen a topic, narrowed it down and specified your objectives (i.e. what you want to find out). Once you have done this, you will be in a position to think about *how* to go about collecting the information you need. Units 6 to 10, which make up this part of the course, cover various methods of collecting the information, or data, which you may need in your investigation.

Unit 6, 'Using and evaluating documentary sources' covers basic skills of analysing and evaluating evidence which you will need no matter what your subject is. In particular, it deals with collecting evidence from written or printed sources, though there are other kinds of 'documents', as you will see. The next four units cover different methods of collecting data from people.

Because you are unlikely to use *all* the research tools covered in this part of the course, we suggest you work through Part 2 like this:

*   If you are doing pure library research, you need only work through Unit 6, and then go on to Part 3.

*   Otherwise, when you have completed Unit 6, we suggest that you *read through* the remaining four units, *whether or not you plan to use all of the methods described*. This is because there is a certain amount of overlap among these units, and also because you may discover a new way of gathering data for your project which you had not thought of.

*   Then go back and work through the unit or units which describe methods which you actually plan to use in your research, doing the reading and activities as you go.

Once you have done this, you will have developed a research tool (or tools) which can be used for data collection.

Assignment 4 asks you to send a copy of the research tool you have devised to your tutor, with some information on how you have designed and tested it, and your plans for using it to gather data. It might be any one, or more, of the following, depending on how you plan to do your research:

• sample questionnaire

• interview schedule

• sample records from library research

• checklists or recording sheets for diary or observation methods.

Your tutor will send you comments, and you can then go on to use this tool to gather data and to analyse it in preparation for the final writing-up stage.

So by the end of Part 2 you should have completed the following stages of your research:

• choosing, developing and testing your research tool(s)

• using it/them to collect data

• initial sorting and analysis of this data.

Part 3 covers the final stage – writing up the final report – but you will need to look ahead at the information about analysing your data, which is included in Unit 11 to check that the data collected using the instruments you design will be easy to analyse.

But before you start on the units in Part 2 and the associated reading in Bell, you should read through the rest of this introduction, which introduces some important principles and concepts.

Some basic principles of collecting data

It was Francis Bacon, writing about the methodology of modern science, who said 'God forbid that we should give out a dream of our imagination for a pattern of the world.' He was setting out a basic principle of research, no matter what its subject: that we should always do our best to present 'things as they are', rather than as we wish they were, or think them to be.

Part 2 of the course is partly about how you can achieve this aim in your own research, and also about how you can check whether other people, whom you are using as sources of information, are presenting you with 'a dream of their imagination' or a true 'pattern of the world'.

Bias or inaccuracy in our research methods is not something we can avoid altogether, but (as Bacon also said) if we are aware of the reasons for bias or error, we can more easily avoid them.

We can identify a number of general reasons for bias or inaccuracy in research:

1   It is impossible to record everything: you have to select.

2   You will notice different features or details depending on the purpose of your research or observation, and what you are looking for.

3   Seeing is an active process: that is, we select and classify automatically as we observe.

4   Features that are important to the researcher are more likely to be remembered and recorded accurately.

There is not much we can do about these sources of bias, except be aware of them. The general point is that selection is inevitable, and that where you have selection, you will inevitably introduce some sort of bias.

However, there are tools which we can use to check that our research is as accurate and complete as possible.

Reliability, validity, representativeness: some tools for evaluating research

How can we guard against bias, and make our data collection more accurate? Social scientists writing about research methods tend to talk about three indicators of accuracy in research:

- reliability
- validity
- representativeness.

What do these terms mean, and how can they help us to make sense of the data we use, and to evaluate the data we produce? Patrick McNeill (1990) provides clear definitions of all three terms, which I am going to use here.

Reliability refers to the *method* of obtaining the information or data, rather than the information itself:

If a method of collecting evidence is reliable, it means that anybody else using this method, or the same person using it at another time, would come up with the same results. The research could be repeated, and the same results would be obtained.

(McNeill 1990:14).

McNeill points out that some methods are considered to be more reliable than others: that is, they are more 'repeatable'.

| Activity 1 | Can you think of any of the research approaches which were introduced in Unit 1 of the course which are unlikely to be considered 'reliable' in this sense? |

The ones I thought of were the case study and the ethnographic style or approach. You may remember that we mentioned a difficulty with both of these methods in making their findings more generalisable. But similar problems could occur with questionnaires, or with interviews.

Validity is about the truthfulness, or accuracy, of the picture presented by the research or data.

Validity refers to the problem of whether the data collected is a true picture of what is being studied. Is it really evidence of what it claims to be evidence of?
(McNeill 1990:15)

Validity can be a particular problem for certain research methods, such as surveys. The example McNeill gives is a survey in which you ask people to fill in a questionnaire to say what they do in their leisure time.

| Activity 2 | Why might this survey produce results which are *reliable*, but not necessarily *valid*? |

The problem which the survey researcher faces is that we cannot tell (without independent evidence, such as observation) whether the answer we get to a question like this really tells us what people do in their spare time (in which case it is valid, or a true answer to the question we are asking) or whether it simply tells us what people say when they are asked this particular question: perhaps because they think we expect a certain kind of answer, or because they find certain kinds of activity more acceptable to admit to than others. (As one of my students put it, 'Well, nobody is going to say they spend their evenings in the pub chatting up men, are they?')

Representativeness is important because, as we have seen, you can never collect all the information possible. Market researchers, or political pollsters, can't ask everyone: they have to select, and attempt to find a sample that is representative. As McNeill explains it, representativeness:

refers to the question of whether the group of people or the situation that we are studying are typical of others. If they are, then we can safely conclude that what is true of this group is also true of others... If we do not know whether they are representative, then we cannot claim that our conclusions have any relevance to anybody else at all. (Ibid.)

Activity 3

Suppose you wanted to find out what Improvements people on a housing estate would like to see in conditions on the estate. You realise you can't ask everyone.

How would you go about getting a representative sample?

What biases might your solutions allow?

Here are some of the things you might have thought of.

You could choose say one house in 10 (or 100) and knock on the doors: but there would be no guarantee that the people in the houses you chose were typical, and this method might underrepresent people who were out in the daytime (or unable/unwilling to come to the door for some reason). You might find it easiest to work through existing community associations: but would these people be typical of the less socially committed members of the community?

Would it be important that your sample take account of the opinions of different age, gender or racial groups? How would you go about doing this?

As you can see, achieving representativeness in your sample isn't necessarily easy. We shall come back to this in Unit 7, on questionnaires and surveys.

But is it meaningful?

Meaningfulness is not a criterion that we often find mentioned in accounts of research methods. But it is perhaps the most important measure of all. If your research is not meaningful, to yourself or to other people, then its other virtues don't really count for much. Research is after all an attempt to paint a picture of the world as it is: to describe it, and often to try to explain some feature of it.

What do we mean by 'meaningful'? The first question is 'meaningful for whom'? In the first place, your research should have some meaning for *you*: it should tackle what C. Wright Mills (1970) calls 'significant problems'. In the second place, it should be meaningful to other people: other researchers in the same field, if you are a student or academic researcher; your clients, funders, other workers who can gain something from your experiences; the community, if you are doing some form of 'action research'.

Activity 4

Think of one example of a book or research study you have read in your research so far which seemed to you meaningful, and one example which seemed not meaningful. What were the differences?

In *The Sociological Imagination*, C. Wright Mills is scathing about what we might call non-meaningful research:

Sometimes ... you may find a book that does not really have any themes. It is just a string of topics, surrounded, of course, by methodological introductions to methodology, and theoretical introductions to theory. These are indeed quite indispensable to the writing of books by men without ideas. And so is lack of intelligibility.

(Mills 1970:238)

Will the information from your research be meaningful? To whom? Why?

Some advice before you get started

Reading

At this point you should read the introduction to Part II in Bell, 'Selecting Methods of Data Collection' (pages 63–66). Use it to review and to add to your knowledge of the principles of reliability and validity which we introduced above.

Notice particularly what Bell says about the possible constraints you will need to keep in mind when designing your research tools (on pages 63–64) and the advice she gives on page 66 about choosing a tool which will help you get answers to the questions that *you* want to ask.

This is, after all, what selecting a research method is all about!

Unit 6: Using and evaluating documentary sources

1   Making sense of data

2   What do we mean by 'documents'?

3   Finding the evidence

4   Evaluating your sources

5   Checklist

6   Suggested reading

1 Making sense of data

[An important part of doing research is checking out the information we have available to us, in order to make certain that the information we put forward ourselves is reliable. This unit looks at the ways researchers evaluate documentary evidence, but the principle is the same, whether the information we receive comes from books, other people or our own observations.]

How do we check out the information we receive?

In our daily lives, we are constantly having to assess the information we receive, whether it comes from the papers we read, the programmes we watch or things we observe or people tell us. We all have a strategy for doing this, which we may not be aware of unless we think about it.

Activity 1

When you read something, or someone tells you something, how do you go about evaluating it for accuracy? What do you do? List all the techniques you can think of.

I would suggest that we judge the information we receive on the basis of our previous experience:

- What is our experience of the thing being described – does what we read or are told fit our own knowledge?

- What do we know about the source of the information – is it what journalists call a 'usually reliable source'?

We do this sort of thing all the time, without really being aware of doing it. Just occasionally, something about the situation may make us aware that we are testing or evaluating the information we receive.

Activity 2

Can you think of examples from your own experience when you were aware of taking particular care to 'check out' information you received? What was the situation?

The sort of things I thought of were:

- when the information was particularly important – for instance, medical information, payment terms for a major purchase like a house or car

- when it seemed likely that the information would be contradictory or less than reliable – in a political debate, perhaps

- when we are in a strange situation and not certain how to interpret the information we receive.

I suspect that it is easier for us to see how we check out or evaluate evidence when we are in a situation where the 'rules' are unfamiliar: a foreign country, for instance.

For example, experience of travelling by bus in Greece has taught me the following rules for evaluating the accuracy of bus timetables:

- A large painted sign at the bus stop is almost certain to be inaccurate.

- A printed timetable is less likely to be correct than a typewritten one, and a handwritten timetable is more reliable than either.

- Timetables entirely in Greek are more reliable than those which include other languages.

- The most reliable source of all is the little old lady in black sitting opposite the bus stop.

What we need to do as researchers is to develop the habit of evaluating all our evidence as though it were 'foreign'. This applies whether we are drawing information from written papers or documents, or from our own observation or other people's. In this unit, we shall be looking particularly at the techniques for evaluating written sources, or documents.

The researcher as historian

For most research projects, you will need to develop the skills of analysing documentary evidence. Sometimes this will be in addition to other methods of gathering information (which are the subject of later units in this part of the course); sometimes – as in historical research, where the subjects are not available to be observed, surveyed or interviewed – it will be the only method.

Activity 3

You may remember that we introduced 'historical research' as a possible approach to your investigation, in Unit 1 of the course. Look back now at your notes on that discussion, and remind yourself of what we said about it.

We said that historical research – and this applies to any research which involves selecting and interpreting documents – is essentially concerned with selecting and evaluating evidence. One advantage is that it can be done at a distance, in space or time, from your subjects: you don't need direct access. It can provide valuable information, but the problems are analysing and interpreting the evidence, and checking it for accuracy and completeness.

2 What do we mean by 'documents'?

Before we begin to talk about using and evaluating documentary evidence, we need to be clear on what we mean by 'a document', and also what types of documents there are which you might use as sources for your investigation.

Reading

Read the introduction to Chapter 6 in Bell, 'The Analysis of Documentary Evidence', and the section headed 'The Nature of Documentary Evidence' (pages 67–69), in which Brendan Duffy, who wrote this chapter, discusses the different kinds of documents researchers may use. Take notes which will help you remember what a 'document' is and the differences between primary and secondary, and between deliberate and inadvertent sources, and between 'witting' and 'unwitting' evidence. You might like to compare your notes with my very brief ones below.

Documents are usually written or printed records, but they can include other media such as audio tape, film, video or photographs. Travers (1964) defines a document as 'an impression left by a human being on a physical object'. (Your research is most likely to be concerned with documents on paper, but don't neglect other relevant sources if they are available to you.)

Primary and secondary sources

Primary sources are those documents which were produced in the period under research. **Secondary sources** are interpretations of events of that period based on primary sources: biographies, histories, textbooks, for example. But as Marwick (1970) points out, one person's secondary source may be another person's primary source – which makes it rather confusing.

Deliberate and inadvertent sources

As their names suggest, 'deliberate' and 'inadvertent' refer to the purpose for which the source was created. **Deliberate sources** are those which were produced for the attention of future researchers. Political diaries are a good example.

Inadvertent sources were not written with the historian or researcher in mind, but for some other, contemporary, purpose. Memos, ordinary letters, handbooks and minutes of meetings are among the examples Duffy gives. Valuable inadvertent sources for other areas of research might include catalogues, posters and advertisements, maps, charts and photographs. Inadvertent sources can be valuable in giving a picture of events as they were seen by participants at the time, though as Duffy warns they still need to be evaluated carefully.

'Witting' and 'unwitting' evidence

Whether the evidence which a document contains is 'witting' or 'unwitting' also depends on the intention of its original author. **'Witting'** evidence is what the author of the document intended to say. **'Unwitting'** evidence is everything else that we can learn from the document. To take a very simple example, I use my computer to write a weekly shopping list. My aim in doing this is to remind me of food and other items that I need to remember to buy. A future historian could, however, use this list to draw all sorts of conclusions, accurate or otherwise, about late-twentieth-century British society, from estimates of household income and the availability of certain foodstuffs, to analyses of the current state of word processor and paper technology.

| Activity 4 | Before you go on, make a list of *all* the kinds of documentary evidence, primary and secondary, that you are likely to need to consult in your research. Your literature search (Unit 4) should have given you some ideas about this. (You are almost certain to need to consult secondary sources at least.) Don't forget to include items like maps and plans, photographs, video or audio recordings if they are available. If you are doing a project in local history, for instance, you may find useful documents like oral history tapes, old maps or photographs in your local library or record office. If you are researching a company or other organisation, you may well need access to the organisation's archives. |

Are the documents you have listed primary or secondary sources? Are they deliberate or inadvertent sources? And is the most important evidence you are likely to glean from them the 'witting' evidence (what the writer intended you to find out) or the 'unwitting' evidence (what you will need to read 'between the lines')?

Finally, how do you plan to go about gaining access to these documents? (You had an opportunity to do some planning in this area in Unit 5, and for Assignment 3, at the end of Part 1.)

3 Finding the evidence

You have already had some practice in locating written sources in the work you did for your literature search in Unit 4, and many of the principles and sources of information are similar when dealing with documents.

Locating documents

Once you have worked out what documents you will need to consult, the next stage, exactly as for the library materials you were searching for in Unit 4, is to find out where they are and how you can get access to them.

Reading

Duffy deals with the question of finding out where the sources you may need are located, and whether you will be allowed to study them, on page 69 in Bell, 'The Location of Documents'.

Read this section now, and note down the actions you are likely to have to take in order to track down documents you need to look at. What if your sources include confidential documents? Will the guidelines on confidentiality which you drew up for Assignment 2 be any help to you in gaining access, or will you simply have to do without that source?

Selecting documents

As with any other kind of evidence, you will have to select on the basis of how much time you have available.

Reading

Duffy gives some guidance on doing this on page 70 in Bell: read this short section, 'The Selection of Documents', now.

Activity 5

If you will be using documentary sources in your research, you should put these principles into practice now, by visiting the library, archive or office which contains your sources. Do a preliminary survey to find out what is available that is of interest to you, and estimate how much time it will take you to go through it.

If time is limited, you may have to be ruthless in selecting a sample of materials for study. Don't forget to take full advantage of any guides to the collection in the form of registers, lists or catalogues of its contents. The person who is responsible for looking after the collection may also be able to guide you to the type of sources you are looking for.

4 Evaluating your sources

When we come to evaluate particular documents, we can distinguish between two sorts of analysis, or criticism: 'external' and 'internal'. It is useful to know about both, though they may not be equally important to us as researchers on small-scale projects.

External criticism: is it genuine and authentic?

It can take considerable expertise to evaluate the genuineness and authenticity of a document, and fortunately you are unlikely to need to make judgements about whether a document is forged for yourself.

But when you examine a document, you should at least try to decide for yourself whether it is what it claims to be, by asking yourself questions like those Duffy suggests on pages 70–72.

| Reading | Read the first part of the section 'The Critical Analysis of Documents' on pages 70–71 in Bell, including the four questions which Duffy uses to evaluate whether a letter, for example, is written by the person who is claimed as its author. |

(Remember, though, that, in the unlikely event that you are dealing with a forgery, the forger will be trying to anticipate questions like these, in order to produce a plausible piece of deception!)

Internal criticism: is it credible?

Authenticity (i.e. whether a document is what it claims to be) is less likely to be a problem for us as researchers than credibility, or bias.

| Reading | Duffy offers three sets of questions on pages 71–72 in Bell, which you can use to check the credibility of a document and its author. |

Try to get in the habit of asking yourself these questions whenever you evaluate a written source, and you will be well on the way to developing your critical skills as a researcher.

Fact or bias?

| Reading | Finish off your reading for this unit by reading pages 72–74 of Chapter 6 in Bell, on how to tell the difference between fact and bias in a document. and on content analysis. Notice that the presence of bias does not necessarily make the document worthless as historical evidence. Notice, too, that you need to be aware of your own possible bias in evaluating any piece of evidence – no matter where it comes from. |

5 Checklist

Using and evaluating documentary sources

1   What sort of documents do you need to look at?

   Are the documents primary or secondary sources?

   Are they deliberate or inadvertent sources?

   Is the 'witting' evidence or the 'unwitting' evidence most important?

2   Locating documents: what, and where, are your sources? Do you need to make any special arrangements for access?

3   Selecting documents: what information do you *really* need?

4   Critical analysis of your sources:

   Are they genuine and authentic: what they claim to be?

   Are they credible?

   What evidence of bias can you detect?

   –   in the sources themselves?

   –   in your own selection and use of sources?

6 Suggested reading

Cohen and Manion (1989) have a chapter on historical research (Chapter 2). Though the examples are aimed particularly at educational researchers, the guidelines on choosing and refining a topic and evaluating your sources would be useful to anyone attempting documents research.

If you are planning to tackle a historical project, you might also like to look at Arthur Marwick's *The Nature of History* (Marwick 1970), which has been used as a basic text for the Open University Arts Foundation course, and in particular at Chapter 5, 'The historian at work'. Later editions (mine is 1976) have added corrections, and have a different pagination from the original. Marwick's other introduction to historical writing mentioned in Bell, *Introduction to History* (Units 3, 4 and 5 of A101, the Arts Foundation Course of the Open University: Marwick 1977) is less likely to be available, as this course has since been replaced; but you might find it in some libraries.

Of the other works mentioned by Duffy in Bell, G. R. Elton's *The Practice of History* (1967) and G. Kitson Clark's *The Critical Historian* (1967) are classics of their kind, both aimed at beginners to professional or academic history.

You will find a different approach to evaluating evidence in *Straight and Crooked Thinking*, Robert H. and Christopher R. Thouless (Thouless and Thouless 1990). The original book by Robert Thouless was first published in 1930, but the latest (fourth) edition has been revised and brought up to date by his grandson. In it, they aim to identify false or illogical statements that get in the way of realistic attempts to evaluate a situation or argument.

Unit 7: Questionnaires and surveys

1 Why do a questionnaire?

2 Who should you ask?

3 Designing the questionnaire

4 Piloting your questionnaire

5 Sending them out, and getting them back

6 Analysis

7 Checklist

8 Suggested reading

Unit 7 is the first of four units in Part 2 in which we look at different ways of getting information from people.

Questionnaires are one of the major tools of the **survey approach** to investigation, which was introduced in Unit 1. A survey, as its name suggests, is a means of getting information about some topic from a relatively large number of people. The most important survey methods, from the point of view of the lone researcher, are questionnaires (which we look at in this unit) and interviews (which are the subject of Unit 8). I suggest you study these two units together, since some of the techniques – for instance, for drawing up questions – are very similar for the two methods.

This unit also introduces aspects of data collection which are relevant to all four of the units on getting information directly from people (Units 7–10). If, for example, your research method involves selecting a sample of people to be investigated from a larger group, you will need to look at Section 2, 'Who should you ask?' And if it involves asking people questions – whether you are planning a questionnaire or interviews – you should look especially at Section 3, on question design.

Because it contains material that is fundamental to all aspects of research involving people, this is an important unit – and also a long one! It will take time to work through it thoroughly and it would be a good idea to take a break part way through.

Surveys are a research method with which most of us will be familiar – as subjects, if not as researchers.

Activity 1	Take a few moments to think about your own experience of questionnaires and surveys. This is most likely to have been as a subject (i.e. the person who is being asked to answer the questions), though you may also have had experience of doing surveys of your own.

How did you find the experience, and what impression do you have of the accuracy of the results?

When recalling your experience of questionnaires and surveys, you may have thought of the census, which is a major survey conducted every 10 years, which aims to cover 100 percent of the population. The method used here is what is called a self-completion questionnaire – the census form is left for you to complete, and collected later.

Another type of survey you are likely to have had experience of is the public opinion poll. This is also a form of questionnaire, but the researcher asks the questions verbally and records your answers. These polls usually fall into one of two categories: political information or market research. Market research is also often conducted using written questionnaires: for instance, the guarantee card for an appliance may include a questionnaire asking you where you bought it and also for details of your lifestyle and buying habits, or a survey form may be printed in a newspaper or magazine, often with a reward for completing and returning it. Hotels, airlines and holiday companies often ask users to complete a questionnaire giving their opinion of the service.

I have to admit that I find surveys and questionnaires like these exasperating. Market researchers always seem to pounce when I am in a rush to get somewhere, and questionnaires never have a box corresponding to my particular lifestyle or opinion of the product!

When I asked students about their experiences of surveys and questionnaires, some of them said that they disliked being approached by researchers, and refused to take part. Some objected to particular questions, for instance about age. A few admitted that they gave deliberately inaccurate or misleading information, e.g. to questions about their voting intentions or what they did in their spare time.

You might like to think about the implications of these responses for the accuracy of survey results – your own included, if you are planning to use a survey, based on either a questionnaire or interviews, as part of your research method.

1 Why do a questionnaire?

Is a questionnaire likely to be a better way of collecting the information you need than other methods: interviews or observation, for example? What are the advantages and disadvantages? If you are not certain about this, it would be a good idea to read quickly through Units 7–10 before you make up your mind about which research methods will suit your investigation best. Then go back and work through the activities for the unit or units on the method(s) you choose.

And before you begin to design a questionnaire of your own, you need to have worked carefully through the stages of planning your research, consulting those who will be involved and clarifying what you need to find out. You should have covered this in Part 1, but now is the time to stop and think again.

What do you need to find out?

Having decided that a questionnaire is an appropriate method, the first thing you need to do is decide exactly what information you hope to obtain from it.

Reading

Read the introduction now to Chapter 7 in Bell, 'Designing and Administering Questionnaires', and then go on to the section 'Exactly What Do You Need to Find Out?', which maps out the first stage in the process of designing your questionnaire (pages 75–76). Bell gives clear instructions as to how to go about this, which I have repeated in the activity below.

Begin by drawing up a preliminary list of questions, as Bell suggests:

1 Look back at the hypothesis, or list of objectives, in your outline, and decide what questions you will need to ask to achieve your objectives, or test your hypothesis.

2 Write down all the possible questions you can think of. Write each question on a separate card or sheet of paper, so that you can change the order and add or remove questions easily.

As you go through the unit, especially Section 3 on designing your questionnaire, you will need to check your draft questions and revise them if you need to. As Bell warns, you will probably need to try out several different wordings to make sure that your questions are clear, say what you intend and are easy to analyse. But spend some time now getting your first thoughts down on paper.

Two simple rules for success

According to Patrick McNeill (1990:18) there are two simple rules for success in designing questionnaires and conducting surveys:

1 choosing the right people to ask

2 having the right questions to ask them.

Of course, he is right: and put like that, it sounds simple. But following these rules can turn out to be complicated in practice. In the next two sections of the unit, we will look at what's involved.

2 Who should you ask?

Having decided that a questionnaire is the right method to give you the information you need for your investigation, and identified the questions you need to find answers to, you need to think about *who* should be asked these questions.

Think about the group of people about whom you want to find information, using your questionnaire. Who are they? How many of them are there? Will you be able to ask everyone in the group to complete the questionnaire, or will you have to select a smaller sample? If so, have you thought about how you will make a selection?

When I applied these questions to a piece of research using questionnaires which I am doing at the moment, I realised that I was relatively fortunate. The project is a pilot survey of the opinions of students on a particular university arts course. I am able to use my own group of about 24 students as a reasonably representative sample of the 300 or so students doing the same course in our region, and hopefully of the several thousand students doing the course in the country as a whole.

You may similarly be planning to conduct your research with a group which is easy to identify and manageable in size. Examples might be: students of a particular year or course of study within a school or college; colleagues within a company site or department; neighbours in a block of flats or a small estate; members of a church or community organisation. But, depending on the topic of your research, it may not be so easy to identify which individuals, in the larger group of possible subjects, you should ask to complete your questionnaire. How do you choose?

For most large-scale surveys (the census is an obvious exception) it is not possible to survey everyone in the survey population. A sample has to be chosen, and the researcher needs to be sure that it is as **representative** as possible, i.e. that the people who are chosen for inclusion in the survey are as similar as possible to those who are not. If it is impossible for you to survey everyone in your target population, you will have to do the same.

Sample size

An obvious question is 'How many people do I have to include in order to have a representative sample?' Roughly speaking, this depends on:

- how big the survey population is in comparison with the sample

- how varied the survey population is.

The general rule is that the larger and more varied the survey population (i.e. the whole group about which you want to find information) the larger the sample should be in order to avoid a particular kind of bias known as sampling error. (You can find a more detailed explanation of this in Cohen and Manion (1989), Chapter 4 – see the Suggested reading at the end of the unit.)

Another general rule of thumb is that a sample smaller than 30 is unlikely to allow you to make useful comparisons, particularly of a statistical nature. If you wish to compare subgroups within the sample, e.g. men vs. women, different age groups, etc., the sample will again need to be larger than if you are treating the entire sample as a whole.

Sampling frame

The first step in selecting your sample is to choose, or produce, a **sampling frame**: that is, a list of the total population to be surveyed, organised into **sampling units** (e.g. individuals, households). A favourite sampling frame for surveys of individual adults, for example, is the electoral register, but for surveys of particular groups, other sampling frames might be more appropriate.

Activity 4

Think of possible sampling frames for the following:

- a study of elderly people living in a geographical area

- a study of juvenile delinquency.

Can you think of any disadvantages of the frames you have chosen?

You may have found this quite tricky. The electoral register doesn't give information about age, and sampling frames based on, for instance, membership in a club for 'senior citizens' or residents of a retirement home might seriously underrepresent other groups of people of a similar age. Similarly, you could presumably use police records for a survey of juvenile delinquents, but this would restrict you to the group of young people who had for one reason or another come to the attention of the police.

Sample types

Having chosen your sampling frame, the next step is to choose the method of selecting your sample group from that frame. Political and market research polls use very sophisticated methods of selecting subjects who are representative, but you are unlikely to need anything that elaborate. Just for information, however, here are the major forms of sampling mentioned by McNeill (1990:36–39). (Once again, you will find additional information, and sample types, in Cohen and Manion (1989:101–104).)

Random sampling is a method in which each member of the group has an exactly equal chance of being chosen: drawing names out of a hat is a simple random sampling method. Quasi-random or systematic sampling is a variation on this: for instance, choosing every tenth name from a list. Strictly speaking, all the names do not have an equal chance of being chosen (depending on their position on the list) but for practical purposes the effect is similar.

Stratified sampling is a method used to take account of possible variations in the sample, in order to make it more representative. For instance, the sample may be divided into women and men, and random sampling techniques used to select a number of subjects of each sex proportional to their numbers in the total population. Stratified sampling might also be used, for instance, to ensure a representative balance in terms of age, or racial or social group.

Quota sampling is a variant, in which subjects are not selected at random from the sampling frame. Instead, the researcher looks for the right number in each category until the quota is filled. This is a common method in market research.

Multi-stage sampling simply means drawing one sample from another. For instance, a national sample of schoolchildren might be drawn from a sample of schools, drawn in turn from a sample of education authorities.

Purposive sampling occurs when a researcher chooses a particular group or place to study because it is the type wanted for the research. Sociologists, for example, may choose to study housewives, or affluent manual workers, because of the particular questions they are trying to answer. Your survey sample may turn out to be purposive for the same reasons.

'Snowball' sampling is a (not particularly systematic) method used in some ethnographic research. The researcher identifies key individuals in a population, and these in turn are asked to suggest others who might also be approached and interviewed.

Reading	Bell has some practical advice on selecting a sample in her chapter on Designing and Administering Questionnaires. Read the section 'Drawing a Sample' on pages 82–84 now.

Activity 5	If your research plan includes a questionnaire or survey for which you will have to select respondents from a larger group, identify:

1   the sampling frame you will use

2   how you are going to select representative subjects for your survey.

---

3 Designing the questionnaire

Once you have decided who should be asked to complete your questionnaire, the next step is to design the questionnaire itself.

As Bell warns in her introduction to Chapter 7, 'It is harder to produce a really good questionnaire than might be imagined.' And she quotes Oppenheim's view (1966:vii) that 'the world is full of well meaning people who believe that anyone who can write plain English and has a modicum of common sense can produce a good questionnaire'. As Bell points out, although plain English and common sense will help, they are not enough to guarantee a good result.

You also need to take care in selecting the question types, in writing the questions, in designing, piloting, distributing and managing the return of your questionnaire. And, importantly, you need to think about how responses to your questions will be analysed *at the design stage*.

In the remainder of the unit, we will work through each of these stages in the process of designing a successful questionnaire.

Question types

Questions can be divided into various categories according to their type, and how structured they are – in other words, how much freedom they give the respondent in his or her reply. The more open or unstructured a question, the more varied the answers are likely to be, and so it may be more difficult to analyse the answer by putting it into a particular category.

More structured questions, or rather, questions which require the respondent to give structured *answers*, will generally be easier to analyse, because the answers will be more predictable. This could be important, especially if you have a large number of questionnaires to analyse or if the aims of your study are quantitative.

Reading	In Chapter 7, Bell uses the seven types of questions identified by Youngman (1986). One of these categories, the **verbal or open** question, is an example of an unstructured question; the others (**list, category, ranking, scale, quantity** and **grid**) are all structured questions of various types.

Read the section 'Question Type' (pages 76–77) now, and make certain that you are clear on the differences among the seven types which Youngman identifies. You might like to try to think of, or find, examples of each type for your notes. (Bell gives examples of list, category, grid and scale questions in Chapter 11.) The next activity will also help you work out how these question types differ.

Activity 6	Look back at the draft questions you drew up for Activity 2. Can you identify the question types you used, from Youngman's list? If you have chosen open questions, can you foresee any problems in analysing the replies? If so, can you rewrite your questions to make them more structured?

Reading	Before you finalise your questions, look ahead to the information on analysing your data in Chapter 11 in Bell, especially the examples of summary sheets you can use to record the answers to your questionnaire on pages 129 and 137. It makes sense to use question types which will make analysis easy, and *at the same time as you design your questionnaire*, you should also design the summary sheet for collecting the data from each questionnaire as it is returned.

Question wording

The actual wording of your questions is one of the most important elements in a successful questionnaire.

Reading	Read the section 'Question Wording' on pages 77–81 in Bell. Here Bell lists some pitfalls to look out for. Read through her description, and then go on to check your own draft questions for the faults she describes.

Activity 7	Check your draft questions. Do they suffer from any of the weaknesses described by Bell? Are they clear and unambiguous, free of assumptions and any wording that could offend your subjects? Have you avoided questions which depend on your subjects' memory, or require specialist knowledge? Any double, leading, presuming or hypothetical questions? Rewrite any that need attention.

The look of it

Particularly if you are sending or leaving your questionnaire for subjects to complete on their own, it needs to be clearly laid out and easy to follow in order to encourage people to fill it in. You don't need to be a specialist on design: if you follow the simple guidelines which Bell gives, and take a little care over presentation, you can produce a questionnaire which will be inviting rather than offputting.

Reading	Read the section 'Appearance and Layout' in Bell (pages 81–82). When you prepare your own questionnaire for distribution, follow the guidelines she gives on layout, spacing and order of questions.

Activity 8	Try to find examples of printed or published questionnaires which you can use to get ideas about question wording, order and layout. These are becoming more and more common, in newspapers and magazines, in postal surveys, on guarantee cards and product registration cards, and so on. You will probably be able to find both good examples and bad!

Then use your models and the guidelines on pages 81–82 in Bell to type or wordprocess a pilot version of your questionnaire. If someone else is doing the typing, make sure you give clear instructions as to just how you want the questionnaire set out.

4 Piloting your questionnaire

You have tried to design a questionnaire which will be easy to follow, with clear and unambiguous questions, which will give you the information you need. The only way to find out whether you have been successful is to try it out on other people, and see whether they find it as clear as you do! Piloting your questionnaire is therefore an important step, even if your sample is a small one.

Reading	Read what Bell has to say about piloting your questionnaire (pages 84–85). The list of questions for you to ask your 'guinea pigs' is particularly useful for sorting out any remaining 'bugs' in your design.

Activity 9	Pilot your questionnaire following the guidelines given by Bell:

1   Ask a small group of people to complete your questionnaire. Ideally they should be similar to your target group, but friends or family will do at a pinch.

2   As soon as possible after they finish the questionnaire, ask them the questions Bell lists on page 85, and use the answers to identify any problems with your questions or the design of your questionnaire. If any questions are left unanswered, or wrongly interpreted, try to find out why.

3   Make any changes that seem necessary before preparing the final version.

5 Sending them out, and getting them back

You now need to think about how you are going to distribute your questionnaire, and also how the replies will come back to you.

Reading	Read the last section of Chapter 7 in Bell, from the heading 'Distribution and Return of Questionnaires' down to the checklist (pages 85–87).

We will come back to some of the later points at the end of the unit. For the moment, concentrate on drawing up a list of things to remember when planning the distribution of your questionnaire.

Here is my list, based on Bell:

1   Make sure that you have permission to distribute your questionnaire to your chosen list of subjects, if this is needed.

2   Choose your method of distribution:

- face-to-face is probably best – you can make contact and explain what you are trying to do

- explore informal distribution methods – colleagues, students, internal mail

- postal surveys are the least desirable distribution method – they are expensive, and have the lowest response rate.

3   If you are not meeting your subjects face-to-face, you will need to include a letter. Your letter should:

- explain the purpose of the questionnaire
- say that permission has been given (if it has)
- explain what protection – confidentiality, anonymity – will be offered
- be neither brusque nor ingratiating in tone
- give a date by which questionnaires should be returned to you:
  - two weeks is about right (more time may mean that the questionnaire is put aside)
  - quote the precise *day and date* to jog people's memories.

4   If the questionnaire will be returned by post, include a stamped self-addressed envelope. (Cohen and Manion suggest that good-quality envelopes, and a first class stamp, will make a good impression.)

Activity 10

Decide what you are going to do about confidentiality, and how you will distribute your forms. Get copies made of your final version, and draft a letter to go with the questionnaire if you will not be distributing it personally.

If you are planning a postal questionnaire, you might like to consult the guidelines in Cohen and Manion (1989) on pages 109–116. They give some useful, and detailed, tips on designing and distributing your questionnaire, though the scale of the survey they seem to have in mind seems rather larger than a lone researcher could be expected to manage!

Non-response

One thing to keep in mind is that you will certainly get some refusals among your chosen sample. The response rate for postal surveys is reckoned to be about 30–40%; face-to-face surveys have a higher rate, of 70% or more. (These figures are based on McNeill (1990:40); Cohen and Manion (1989:114) are more optimistic, especially about surveys where a follow-up is possible.)

The question, of course, is 'Are those who answer survey questions different from those who refuse?' Unfortunately, the answer seems likely to be yes, as Bell reports. It will certainly improve the validity of your results if you can get replies from as many of your subjects as possible.

Notice that there is a problem here, if you have decided to offer respondents anonymity. But if you are able to identify those who have not replied, send out a reminder letter and duplicate questionnaire about a week after your original return date, so that stragglers do not delay the analysis stage.

Activity 11

Decide what you are going to do about follow-up. Will it be possible to code responses so that you can identify non-respondents, or is anonymity more important to your research design?

Send out reminder letters if appropriate.

6 Analysis

As Bell remarks (page 87), it is best to wait if you can until all questionnaires (or as many as you seem likely to get) are returned, before you begin to code and record them. But if time is limited, you may need to begin recording responses as soon as the first questionnaires are returned.

Unit 11 below and Chapter 11 in Bell, give more detailed guidance on how to analyse your results. You should look at them before you start the job of recording.

7 Checklist

Use the 'Questionnaire Checklist' on pages 87–89 in Bell to make sure that you have not left anything out, as you work through the stages of preparing and distributing your questionnaire.

8 Suggested reading

McNeill (1990) has a useful chapter on surveys (Chapter 2, 'Social surveys') which I have drawn on, especially for the section on sampling.

Cohen and Manion (1989) also have a chapter (Chapter 4) on surveys, which gives detailed guidance on question design and layout, sampling techniques and organising a postal questionnaire. There are also examples of the use of survey research in education.

For more detailed guidance on analysing your survey, and especially the use of statistical techniques, see the Suggested reading section at the end of Unit 11 below.

Unit 8: Interviews

Interviewing is a skill which can be developed into a highly sophisticated tool, but it is based on a very simple idea. If you:

- display an interest in, and respect for, people

- ask uncomplicated questions

- listen

- record what is said

you will gain a great deal of valuable material. Simple it may be, but for a variety of reasons, many people do not follow these basic 'rules'.

But even a simple interview needs planning.

| Activity 1 | The process of planning interviews is in many ways similar to planning a questionnaire. Think back to your work on Unit 7. |

What kinds of things will you need to decide, and do, in order successfully to conduct an interview or a series of interviews? Jot down all the points you can think of.

I came up with a list which seemed to sum up the planning stages:

1   Decide what sort of information you are looking for. Is an interview the best method? If so, what kind of interview should you go for?

2   Choose your interviewees.

3   Arrange for the interviews to take place.

4   Work out the questions you are going to ask, and decide how you are going to record the interview.

5   Conduct the interview.

6   Record your findings.

Let's take these stages in turn.

1 Interview or questionnaire?

One way of looking at the advantages and disadvantages of the interview method of gathering information about people is to compare it with another method which we have already looked at – the questionnaire.

Read the introduction to Chapter 8 in Bell (pages 91–92) and note the pros and cons of using interviews rather than a questionnaire to gather information.

Bell has more to say about one major disadvantage of interviews at the end of the chapter. Read the section 'A Few Words of Warning' (pages 98–99) before you take the final decision to include interviews in your research.

It seems to me that the main advantage of the interview over the questionnaire is that it is more flexible: it allows you to follow up or explain questions, and to gain information from the way in which a subject responds, which you cannot do with a questionnaire. Questions do not need to be worded quite so carefully, either, though Bell does warn that careful preparation is still important.

The biggest disadvantage is probably the time interviews take, which means that you will not be able to interview as many people as you could reach with a questionnaire. You will also need to be able to arrange interviews at times which suit your interviewees, and allow time for travel, and for missed appointments or cancellations, as well as time to write up your notes or transcribe tapes. If you are planning to use interviews as part of your research method, you will need to make certain that you have time in your schedule to deal with all this. You can use the estimates Bell gives on pages 98–99 to work out how many interviews you can manage in the time you have available.

2 What sort of interview?

Once you have decided that an interview is the best method of finding out what you need to know, you will need to choose the type of interview which is most likely to produce the information you are looking for. At one extreme is the completely structured or formal interview, where the interviewer is as neutral as possible, and generally uses a questionnaire-like checklist to record responses. (You will find an extract from such a checklist, or interview schedule, on page 93 in Bell). Market research interviews are an example of this type. At the other end of the scale is the completely unstructured or informal interview, more like an ordinary conversation, in which the shape of the interview is determined by how interviewees respond to your questions.

Your choice will depend in part on what you want to find out. If it is important for interviewees to be able to put forward their own opinions, and say what they think is important, or if you are not sure yet what the important issues are, you will tend to choose a more informal approach. On the other hand, if you are seeking specific pieces of information, and want to be able to compare responses from different individuals, and quantify your results, you will need to use a more structured technique.

As Bell points out, for an inexperienced interviewer working to a tight deadline, the formal or structured interview has certain advantages: it is more straightforward to conduct, and the results will be easier to analyse. But you will need to take a decision depending on your skills, the time you have available, and what you need to find out. You may even decide to combine different types of interviews, at different stages of your research.

Read what Bell has to say about the different types of interview, and the advantages and disadvantages of each, in the section 'Type of Interview' (pages 92–95). Notice that in addition to the two types I mentioned above, the formalised or structured interview and the informal interview, she mentions two other types which may be of interest to you: the preliminary interview, in which the purpose is to find out what the major issues are for your interviewees, and which therefore needs to be as unstructured as possible, and the guided or focused interview, which is somewhere between the two extremes, and which may seem to you to have the best of both worlds.

When you have read the section, use the information in it to take a decision about the type (or types) of interview that will be best for you to use.

Activity 2

Think about the type of interview which will be best in your case. Is it important to have certain standard items of information from each interviewee, or are people's freely expressed beliefs or opinions more important? Would it be a good idea to plan a small number of informal preliminary interviews with selected respondents, to identify important themes and topics for your research?

3 Planning the interview

Preparing for interviews is much the same as for questionnaires, as we saw in Activity 1. You will need to:

- decide who to interview
- make contact with your interviewees, and arrange for the interview to take place
- work out what questions you want to ask, and in what order
- pilot your interview schedule
- conduct the main interviews, using a method of recording that suits you
- write up your findings.

Choose your interviewees

You now have to think about who you know, or could make contact with, who could help you find the information you need to answer the questions you raised in your outline.

Activity 3

Whom do you plan to interview? Do you have particular individuals in mind, or simply members of a particular group? How can you go about making contact? Will you need permission from anyone apart from the interviewees themselves?

Spend some time drawing up a strategy, and decide whom you will need to approach. On a small project with a short timescale, you may not be able to interview as many people you would like, or select a true random sample.

Remind yourself of what Bell has to say about choosing a sample on pages 82–84.

Arrange for the interviews to take place

Depending upon the people you have chosen, you may be able to approach them directly for permission, or you may have to obtain permission from someone of authority in the organisation first.

Here are some things to think about when setting up your interviews:

- Before you make any appointments, make sure that official channels have been cleared. If necessary, ask your supervisor, or someone in authority in your own organisation, for a letter of authorisation which you can send or give to possible interviewees.
- Remember that the interviewee is doing you a favour: the time and place of the interview need to be arranged to suit his or her convenience, not yours!
- Arrange a place to meet where the interviewee will be at ease, which is quiet and private, and where you are not likely to be interrupted.
- When you make the appointment, say how long the interview is likely to last – and do your best not to go over this limit.
- Remember it is almost always best to be alone with a single interviewee. Group interviews are for special purposes only.

Activity 4

Use the above guidelines to make arrangements for interviews with the subjects you have chosen. Look back at Unit 5, and the checklist at the end of Chapter 5 in Bell (pages 58–59) to remind you of what needs to be done when negotiating access. You will need to prepare copies of the explanatory note describing the study and explaining your policy on confidentiality and anonymity, which you did for Assignment 3, to give to participants.

Work out the questions to ask

This is potentially one of the most important stages in planning a successful interview, though, as we have seen, it may not be quite as important to be precise about your wording as it is for questionnaires.

If you are planning a structured interview, you will need to prepare an interview schedule, with questions in the order you want to ask them and prompts to remind you of the information you are looking for in each case. (Have another look at the example on page 93 in Bell, of part of an interview schedule for the project on mature students.) If the interviews will be unstructured or focused, you will need to be clear what topics you plan to cover; and you will still need some sort of checklist to make certain that nothing vital is left out.

Here are some more points to keep in mind when drawing up your questions, especially for less formal interviews:

- Use questions that give your interviewee a chance to say more than just 'Yes' or 'No'.

- Avoid complex and double-barrelled questions – you will only get half an answer.

- Unless you require some specific fact, use open-ended questions such as 'Could you please describe …', and 'What do you think about …'.

- Avoid leading questions – giving an opinion can easily distort the interview.

- Try to phrase questions so that people reply in their own way. Avoid questions which make people think in your way.

Activity 5

Work out whether you plan to conduct a structured or unstructured interview, and draw up the list of questions you plan to ask. You might like to look back at the rules laid down for questionnaire design in Unit 7.

Bell gives you a reminder of these rules on page 92. As for questionnaires, prepare your topics and questions on cards or separate sheets of paper, so that you can decide the order once all the topics have been covered. Follow the same rules (no leading, presumptive or offensive questions, etc.). Think about what is likely to be the best order in which to ask questions. The order may be important in establishing an easy relationship with the interviewee: for instance, it is again a good idea to leave sensitive questions until late in the interview, once a rapport has (hopefully) been established.

Once you have finalised your list of questions, write them down in the order you want to ask them.

It is a good idea to pilot your interview questions, partly to gain practice in the technique of conducting interviews. The *way* in which you ask questions can have as important an effect on the interview as the questions themselves. So, if you can, try out your questions on a friend, colleague or fellow student, to see if they are clear and to check that you have an appropriate interview 'style'. Piloting your schedule will also give you confidence, and give you the opportunity to practice recording answers as you conduct the interview.

Before you conduct your first interview, you will need to take a decision on how to record your findings. Look ahead at Section 5 of this unit, and the section 'Recording and Verification' in Bell (page 96) if you are not certain how to go about this.

4 Conducting the interview

As Bell points out (pages 96–97), conducting an interview is really a matter of using normal good manners and common sense, though there are one or two particular points to keep in mind:

It is difficult to lay down rules for the conduct of an interview. Common sense and normal good manners will, as always, take you a long way, but there are one or two courtesies that should always be observed. You should always introduce yourself and explain the purpose of the research, even if you have an official introductory letter. Make it quite clear what you will do with the information and check whether quotations and views must be anonymous or whether they can be attributed.

Here are some more rules to keep in mind, which should help your interviews run smoothly:

Always explain in a simple way what the interview is for – and how the informant can help. Be open about intentions and honour any promises.

LISTEN – remember the effect of chattiness is usually to shut people up. An interview is not a conversation – the whole point is to get the informant to speak.

Ask no more questions than are needed.

Adopt a clear, simple and unhurried manner. If you are not clear about what to ask next, remember a pause is better than confusion.

Never interrupt a story – if there is a digression use a phrase at the 'end' like 'Earlier you were saying ...'.

Be flexible – you may gain more by running with the person's flow than by sticking closely to your preferred order or, indeed, areas.

MAKE NOTES AS YOU GO.

Remember that it is your responsibility to keep to the time limit you originally agreed with the interviewee. Keep an eye on the time – but be careful not to put the interviewee off.

Try not to rush away immediately after the interview – allow time to chat. Your interviewee is likely to want some feedback on what has been said and to know more about the context in which it is to be used.

Check your notes with the interviewee for accuracy.

Be polite – thank the interviewee before you leave.

Johnson (1984) makes the point strongly that it is the responsibility of the interviewer, not the interviewee, to end an interview. She writes:

It may have been difficult to negotiate access and to get in in the first place, but the interviewer who, once in, stays until he is thrown out, is working in the style of investigative journalism rather than social research ... If an interview takes two or three times as long as the interviewer said it would, the respondent, whose other work or social activities have been accordingly delayed, will be irritated in retrospect, however enjoyable the experience may have been at the time. This sort of practice breaks one of the ethics of professional social research, which is that the field should not be left more difficult for subsequent investigators to explore by disenchanting respondents with the whole notion of research participation.

(Johnson 1984:14–15, quoted in Bell, page 97)

The problem of bias

I said earlier that the way in which you ask your questions can have as important an effect on the interview as the questions themselves. [Bias is a particular problem for interviewers, especially those who are seeking quantifiable results, because two human beings are involved, and this inevitably brings in an element of unpredictability.]

Many factors can influence your interviewees' responses, one way or another. If you appear friendly and pleasant, your respondent may change his or her replies, and so distort the results, because of eagerness to please you; conversely, antagonism between interviewee and interviewer will also affect the results. According to McNeill (1990:39), 'friendly but restrained' is the phrase professional surveyors use to describe the ideal interviewer. There will be other factors, such as your sex, race, age or accent, which may affect how the interviewee will perceive you, which you can do less about – you can only try to be aware of the possible effect this may have on your results.

If you are an 'inside researcher', you may find yourself in the difficult position of interviewing colleagues, and perhaps senior colleagues, about their work. This can be an uncomfortable situation for both parties. On page 98, Bell quotes the experience of a teacher who had to interview his headmaster about the school's management policy, as part of his research. Here again, there is little you can do apart from being aware of the situation.

Particularly if you feel strongly about the issues you are researching, there is also a danger that you may try to 'lead' the interview, by seeking answers that support your preconceived ideas.

Survey researchers call these influences 'response effect' or 'interviewer effect'.

Perhaps the most important safeguard against bias is to be aware of the problem.

Reading

Read what Bell has to say about the problem of bias in interviews, and the difficulties which interviewers can face. You will find information about this in the section headed 'Bias' on pages 95–96.

Take time to think about how the problem of bias may affect the interviews you are planning.

5 Recording your findings

Recording your interview on the spot is essential – it both demonstrates your interest in what is being said and means that less material gets lost.

The only question is, how should you record? If you are conducting structured interviews, with an interview schedule, it will probably be easy to mark responses on the sheet and scribble in any additional comments which strike you as worth recording.

An informal interview will be more difficult to record in this way, since it will not be as easy to predict what your respondent will say. Pen and paper is still probably best, however – if you are not used to interviewing, tape recorders tend to add to your nerves, and may also make your interviewees less willing to talk openly. Transcribing tapes can also be a very lengthy process, unless you have access to secretarial help, as Bell points out.

Reading

Read what Bell has to say about the advantages and disadvantages of the different methods of recording, in the section 'Recording and Verification' (page 96), before you take a final decision on the method of recording you will use. You will see that in general she is inclined to prefer pen and paper methods over tape recording.

It goes without saying that you should always ask permission to tape record an interview. Notice too Bell's warning about the importance of clearing interview transcripts and statements with your sources, particularly if you want to use direct quotations.

My own experience of recording interviews, and that of my husband, who is a technical journalist, suggests that your choice will depend in part on your own skills and how much detail you need to record. I have found tapes very valuable in recording interviews where it was important to me to have details of the conversation, and to reproduce exactly the interviewee's own words – for instance, in a series of interviews which I used to develop case study material for management training. More structured interviews worked perfectly well with a schedule on which I could mark responses and add comments.

My husband also tends to tape record major interviews in which detail is important: he says that this allows him to concentrate on the questions he wants to ask and the way in which the interviewee responds. He also finds that the tape records technical details which his notes do not, and which he may not have remembered accurately. For less formal interviews, at exhibitions for instance, he will use the classic reporter's notebook and his own form of shorthand. He finds, though, that people are less willing to answer sensitive questions if a tape is running – even if they are told that they can push the 'stop' button at any time and go 'off the record'. The least successful recording method was a one-handed word processor which he used a few years ago. It was faster than note-taking by hand, but people were so fascinated by this strange device that they became speechless!

Whatever method you use, but particularly if you are taking notes by hand, it's important to go over your record of the interview as soon as possible afterwards, before your memory of what was said fades. You may be surprised at how much additional detail you can recall if you do this immediately. So:

- After the interview, record as quickly as possible any additional comments of your own.
- Make sure your material is clearly labelled.
- Reread the material – make notes on major points and list things that require further exploration.

Particularly if you intend to use interviews as a major, or only, method of research, it is worth spending a little time reading what other researchers have written. See the Suggested reading list in this unit for this. But remember that in the end you will only learn how to conduct a useful interview by doing it.

When you have finished your reading, conducted a few trial interviews, piloted your schedule and thought about how you will analyse the responses, you will be ready to proceed with your interviews.

Use the guidelines above and in Bell (especially the 'Interview Checklist' on pages 99–101) to conduct and record the interviews you need for your research. Remember to keep a copy of your interview schedule to include in Assignment 3, at the end of Part 2 of the course.

6 Checklist

Use the 'Interview Checklist' on pages 99–101 in Bell if you will be using interviews as a research technique for your investigation.

7 Suggested reading

Cohen and Manion (1989) have a useful chapter on 'The Interview', including a table summarising the relative advantages of interview and questionnaire, examples of questions from interview schedules, and suggestions on how to code your responses (Chapter 13, pages 307–335).

Chapter 11, 'Conducting and Analysing Interviews', in Bell *et al. Conducting Small-Scale Investigations in Educational Management* (1984), is another useful account. The article by Daphne Johnson quoted above, 'Planning Small-scale Research' (Johnson 1984), is also in this collection, and worth reading.

Unit 9: Diaries and other records of time use

1   The diary as a research tool
2   Who can you ask?
3   What information?
4   Other methods: critical incident recording and problem portfolios
5   Checklist

This unit covers several related methods of finding out what people do, which can be loosely grouped together as diary methods. As well as various forms of diaries proper, we consider two other methods of investigating how your subjects use their time: critical incident recording and the problem portfolio method.

1 The diary as a research tool

When you think of a diary, you probably have in mind either the book in which you record engagements, or a personal journal. The diary as a research tool is neither of these, though the common denominator is that a research diary also focuses on the way in which people use time. This is also what the diary has in common with critical incident recording and problem portfolio methods, which are specific ways of looking at what people do, usually in their work, during a certain period of time.

You can use the diary technique to identify your own use of time. Managers are often encouraged to keep a job diary, for instance, in order to see what they spend most time doing, and to make their use of time more productive. But in general this method refers to asking *other people* how they use their time, in more or less detail. The diary may be general, asking subjects to provide an account of their working day, for instance, or it may be specific, e.g. a log of television watching or shopping habits.

Diaries can be used in combination with interviews (Unit 8) or with observation studies (Unit 10) to provide information about the behaviour of individuals and groups. Unlike interviews and questionnaires, which can be used to ask about people's feelings and opinions, diaries provide information to answer the question 'What happened?'

Benefits and problems of diary research

Reading

In her introduction to Chapter 9, 'Diaries', and in a short paragraph at the very end of the chapter, Bell introduces the main features of the diary method, and discusses the problems associated with research using diaries. Read these passages now to identify possible uses for diary methods, as well as possible problems, and to get a general picture of the methods used.

Activity 1

You might like to stop at this point and think about whether you have ever had the experience of keeping a diary in the research sense – that is, a record of how you used your time, or of particular activities you took part in.

If you have had an experience like this, how did you find it? Were there any difficulties you can recall, which might make the method difficult to use for research?

If you have taken part in certain kinds of professional or management training courses, for instance a course in time management, you may have been asked to keep a time use diary, recording exactly how you used your time for a day or a week. If you were conscientious in keeping this up, it may have struck you that you were spending quite a lot of time recording what you did. If you were less conscientious, and filled up your sheets from memory at the end of the day or week, you may have wondered how much you had forgotten about the details.

I can recall once being asked to keep a record of our television watching, as a household, for a week. This was simple to do – all we had to do was list the programmes we watched, with the time and date, on a form. But I can recall the temptation to watch programmes, and in particular certain kinds of programmes, in order to have something worthwhile to record. In fact, we watched very little television that week, which was probably typical, but it is still possible that we were behaving differently because of the task we had been given. Oppenheim (1966, quoted on page 102 in Bell) makes precisely this point.

Diaries can be used in a variety of ways, and in combination with, or as a substitute for, other methods. One possible use for diaries is as a preliminary to interviewing. As Bell reports (on pages 103–104), Zimmerman and Wieder (1977) used them in this way and suggest that they are particularly useful in cases where it may not at first be clear what are the right questions for the interviewer to ask. A study of the diary may give valuable clues:

the diarist's statement is used as a way of generating questions for the subsequent diary interview. The diary interview converts the diary – a source of data in its own right – into a question-generating and, hence, data-generating device.

(1977: 489, quoted in Bell, page 104)

As Bell notes, Zimmerman and Wieder also found the use of a diary, in conjunction with the diary interview, useful as a substitute for the method of participant observation (which I introduced in Unit 1 as the ethnographic style of research). They reported that their method overcame some of the disadvantages of the participant observer method, such as the length of time needed and the danger that people's behaviour is changed by the presence of an observer.

However, diaries have their disadvantages too, and it is important to be aware of these before deciding on this method:

1   Keeping a diary is time-consuming for the subjects, and briefing and encouraging your sources may be time-consuming for you as researcher.

2   Because of the commitment needed, it may be difficult to find (enough) people willing to get involved, or willing to complete the exercise: the refusal and dropout rates may be high.

3   Subjects need to be relatively well-educated, and committed to keeping an accurate record, if the diary is to be useful as a research tool. If people fail to understand what they are asked to do, or lack the motivation to keep the diary regularly, the information provided will be much less valuable.

4   The need to record behaviour may cause the subject to modify the behaviour we want to find out about.

This is a major potential problem with the diary method; you will remember Oppenheim's concern (Bell, page 102) that 'the respondent's interest in filling up the diary will cause him to modify the very behaviour we wish him to record'.

Do you need to use the diary method?

The limitations of the diary method – in particular the time involved, and the need to brief participants carefully and check on their progress during the diary period – need to be balanced against the difficulty of obtaining the same information in other ways. For instance, you can ask people in an interview how they spend their time, but the answer is less likely to be accurate, because people forget, or are unaware of how much time, for instance, they spend on unproductive activities.

There are times, then, when the diary will be the best, or even the only, method, of finding out what you need to know. So there is no reason not to use diaries in your research, as long as you recognise the problems, and are confident you can overcome them.

<table>
<tr><td>

Activity 2

</td><td>

Think about whether any of the questions you are trying to answer for your investigation are appropriate for the diary method. Do you need to find out, for instance:

- what people actually do over a period of time, either generally or in some specific area of their lives?
- how people use their time, or how much time they spend on a particular activity or activities?
- the pattern of work or other activities within an organisation?
- what people see as the most important uses of their time?

Jot down the information you think diaries might give you.

</td></tr>
</table>

Assuming that you decide to use the diary method, or a related method like the critical incidents or problem portfolio technique, as one of your research tools, the basic questions are the same as for the questionnaire or interview:

- Who will you ask to complete your diary?
- What questions will you ask them?

2 Who can you ask?

In thinking about who can be asked to keep a diary for your project, you need to think about:

- who can give you the information you need
- who will be willing to get involved.

As Bell points out in her analysis of the pros and cons of the diary method, diarists need to be of a certain educational level to understand the instructions and complete the diary correctly. They must also have time, and be prepared to stop what they are doing at intervals to fill in a form or make a note of an activity. If they are not sufficiently motivated, they will probably fill the forms in carelessly, or not at all.

This means that, if you are asking friends, neighbours or colleagues to go to the trouble of keeping a diary, you need to be very sure that this is the best way of obtaining the information you want. And you will need to convince your subjects of this as well – and make them see that their cooperation will be valuable in some way. Otherwise, it is better to choose a different method.

<table>
<tr><td>

Activity 3

</td><td>

If you have decided that asking certain individuals to keep a diary would help you in your research, you may well have taken that decision with particular individuals in mind. If not, ask yourself the two questions below.

1 Who can give me the information I need by keeping a diary for a period of time?

2 How can I persuade people that my investigation is worthwhile, and that they should give the time to help me?

</td></tr>
</table>

You will also need to think about how long you will need to ask subjects to keep the diary, and what you will ask them to record. We will deal with these questions in Section 3 of the unit.

Getting permission

Remember that, as with any form of research involving other people, you will need to get permission from the people involved, and also if necessary from someone of authority in the organisation.

It is also essential to meet the people who will be giving up their time, so that you can explain the purpose of the exercise fully, inquire about likely problems and, if possible, resolve them.

Explaining what you want

Moser and Kalton (1971:340–341) suggest that using the diary method will probably involve several visits to the people taking part.

They consider that you need at least one visit to gain the subject's cooperation and to explain the recording procedure. If you have prepared a diary sheet for participants to fill in, you will need to hand it over and give instructions on how it should be used. These will need to be clear and explicit, as Bell warns on page 81.

You may need to arrange a second interview at the end of the recording period, to collect the diary and to go through it with respondents to check that they have used it in the way you anticipated, and to resolve any queries.

In between, Moser and Kalton suggest that it is a good idea to make other visits, or perhaps phone calls, to check that the instructions have been understood and that data are being correctly recorded, and also to keep up your subjects' morale.

Diaries are not a quick method, for you or for your respondents, and you need to keep this in mind when deciding whether this approach is for you.

3 What information?

As well as thinking about who should be asked to complete a diary, you also need to think about what you will ask your subjects to do. Will you ask them to use their own categories to describe events, or give them a checklist? For how long a period will you ask them to keep the diary, and how often will they be asked to make entries?

There are advantages and disadvantages to both the checklist and the 'free hand' approaches to diary recording, and you will need to make up your mind depending on what is important to you. If you give your subjects the freedom to devise their own system of recording, you will get a clearer picture of how they see things, but it may be more difficult to analyse the information and to compare diary entries from different subjects. If you provide the categories, subjects may interpret them differently. but at least you will have the basis for analysis and comparison.

Two contrasted methods used by researchers may give you an idea of the possibilities.

Reading

Read the accounts in Bell of the way in which diaries were used to gather information by Zimmerman and Wieder (1977) and Bradley and Eggleston (1976). Notice that Zimmerman and Wieder asked their diarists to describe what they did in their own words, using the formula what/when/where/how, while Bradley and Eggleston used a form or checklist.

Activity 4

If you are thinking of using a diary form in your research, try keeping it yourself for at least one day, just to give yourself an idea of the sort of time commitment you will be asking of your subjects. If the categories are not appropriate for the sort of work you do, try identifying categories for your own working day or leisure activities and again use them to record your use of time for a day or a week.

You are likely to discover for yourself that completing a diary can be time-consuming, and that there are difficulties in deciding what category an action belongs in, and how many minutes have been spent on particular types of activity.

Designing your categories

Activity 5

Decide how much guidance you are going to give your subjects on what to record, and if necessary draw up a diary checklist, form or grid.

You might find it useful to look again at the information in Units 7 and 11, and the associated chapters in Bell, on devising questions and on analysing your data once you have collected it. You should also look at Section 4 below, to make certain that the methods described there are not more appropriate for your study than the diary proper.

Before you try out your system on others, go through the procedure you will ask your subjects to follow, at least for a short period.

As with all data-collecting instruments, your diary should be piloted to make sure that participants are clear about what they have to do, and that the information the diary provides will be useful to you. At the pilot stage, ask yourself again what you will do with the information you receive. You will be putting participants to a great deal of trouble: will it be worth it? Could you obtain the same information from questionnaires, or from short interviews? If so, perhaps the diary is not the best method to use.

However, if you decide that it really is what you need, revise your checklist or instructions using the information from your pilot, and go on to the main phase of your research.

How much time?

As well as deciding the topics and categories to be covered, you will need to think about how long you can ask your subjects to keep the diary. Remember that a detailed diary, in which information needs to be entered several times a day or even several times an hour, can probably only be kept up reliably for a day or a few days at a time; a more general diary, which asks people to record the day's events in broad categories and time blocks, will be less time-consuming and can probably be kept up for longer.

Your pilot subjects should be able to give you some guidance about the amount of time they actually took to complete the diary, and any problems they had (for instance, deciding in which category a particular activity belonged), and you can adjust the final version to take account of this if necessary.

You will, of course, have to hope that the day, or week, in which your subjects are completing their diary exercise is typical. You may be able to get some idea of how representative your chosen period was by asking your subjects when you collect the completed diaries or diary forms.

4 Other methods: critical incident recording and problem portfolios

A diary can provide very detailed information about the subject's activities during a day, week, month or whatever. But you may not need such detailed information. If what you really need to know is the type of problems your subjects encounter in their work, or key aspects of their daily life or job, the critical incidents or problem portfolio methods may be more suitable than the ordinary diary.

The critical incidents method is another way of investigating a pattern of activities, especially in connection with work, in which people are asked to describe what 'critical incidents' occurred during a specified period of time.

Reading

Read the account in Bell (pages 105–107) of the critical incidents and problem portfolio methods, which is based on Oxtoby's account of his research (1979) into the problems facing heads of department in further education. Notice Oxtoby's comparison of his chosen method with other possibilities. He concludes that some methods, such as interviews, questionnaires and observation, are obviously not suitable for people trying to monitor their *own* activities, and that others, like job diaries, are time-consuming, often inaccurate and may be difficult to use as a basis of comparison. Note why he thinks that critical incident and problem portfolio methods seem more suitable.

Notice that Bell, too, identifies two advantages of the critical incident/problem portfolio methods over the normal diary:

- they do not require your subjects to spend time recording trivial items
- they allow you to see what the subjects themselves consider to be significant issues or problems.

As with the diary, you may wish to provide a checklist or grid to help subjects record features of the critical incidents or problems they identify. And, as before, you will need to make sure that your instructions are clear and that you are not asking participants to take on such a demanding task that they are likely to abandon it partway through.

Activity 6

If you decide to use a critical incident or problem portfolio method with your subjects, you will need to decide how to ask them for information. You might, like Oxtoby, ask them to identify a single event, e.g. 'the most difficult task or situation' which they have had to face during the past few days or a week. Or you might prefer, as Marple suggests, to ask your subjects to keep a 'problem portfolio' recording problems they had to face each day, how they arose, and what they did. As always, work out what you need to know and try to devise a question or procedure that will give you the information you want, as accurately as possible.

5 Checklist

Use the 'Diaries and critical-incidents Checklist' on pages 107–108 in Bell to decide whether you are going to use diary methods for your research, and to take you through the planning stages.

Unit 10: Observation studies

Up until now, the methods we have described for getting information about people have been indirect, involving some form of questioning people about their activities, opinions or beliefs. There is of course a more direct way of finding out information about other people, which is the subject of this unit. Put briefly, you can watch them to see what they do. Observation is a good method for revealing what *actually* happens, for instance in interactions between individuals in a group, rather than what people *think* is happening.

It is perhaps worth saying, though, that observation methods can only reveal what you, the observer, think or perceive is happening, and your observations, like those of your subjects, may not, indeed cannot, be entirely accurate, complete and free from bias.

This unit, then, is about watching, or observing, people as part of your research. We begin by considering the advantages and disadvantages of the observation (sometimes called participant observation) method, and go on to describe a variety of ways in which you might record your observations and analyse the results.

| Activity 1 | Observation is a method which, like all the others, has drawbacks as well as benefits. Can you think of any? Think particularly of the situation in which you are observing people, or a situation, which you know well – for instance, in your own organisation or neighbourhood. Jot down some notes. |

Once you have thought about this, compare your notes with the difficulties which Bell mentions in her introduction to Chapter 10, 'Observation Studies'. Read the first section of the chapter now, and note down what these difficulties are and how they might affect you if you plan to use observation methods in your research.

| Reading | Read the introduction to the Chapter 10 in Bell (pages 109–111) down to the heading 'Recording and Analysing'. Will you be a participant or non-participant observer in the situations you plan to observe? What difference might this make to your research? |

1 What are you going to focus on?

Whether you are a participant or non-participant observer, the first decision you have to make, before you can choose a method of recording your observation, is what the focus of your research will be.

As Bell explains (pages 111–112) there are a number of ways of recording what happens, say, in a classroom or at a meeting, but before you can choose a method, you need to decide exactly what to observe. The point is that it is impossible to record everything, and the recording method you choose will be different, depending on the focus of your observation.

As we have said already, observation is a particularly good method for revealing what actually happens in interactions between individuals in a group. The techniques for recording which we discuss in this unit are generally designed to record verbal interactions, for instance in a meeting, in terms of either **content** or **process**. If you want to do other types of observation studies – for instance of the behaviour of people in a public place, when you cannot hear what is being said and cannot identify the individuals, or even of the behaviour of animals – you will need to devise different categories, but the principles are the same.

<table>
<tr><td>

Activity 2

</td><td>

First decide what sort of activity you plan to observe – a meeting, a classroom session, a group discussion. What plans will you need to make in order to gain access to the group or situation as an observer?

Next, you will need to decide what interests you. Is it

- the content of the meeting or discussion, i.e. *what* is said?

Or is it

- the process, for instance:
  - the interactions between individuals
  - the number and nature of the contributions made by participants
  - another specific aspect, such as questioning techniques?

</td></tr>
</table>

2 Methods of recording and coding your data

<table>
<tr><td>

Reading

</td><td>

Once you have decided what sort of information you are interested in gathering, read the long section in Bell headed 'Recording and Analysing' (pages 111–116) and take notes on the different methods of recording observations which she discusses. There are some useful examples of the different recording methods which you can use as models in drawing up your own charts and checklists.

</td></tr>
</table>

The methods Bell discusses are:

Video and audio recording

Video recording in particular is likely to be beyond the means of a single-person research project – though the technology is getting cheaper all the time. Keep in mind, too, the time needed to go back through tapes and transcribe or analyse their contents. This method can be expensive in time, as well as money!

Interaction-process analysis

This is a method of recording which seeks to identify classes or categories of behaviour likely to take place in meetings or other group events, and record the number of times individuals display these behaviour types. Letter or number codes may be used as shorthand for different classes of behaviour, and there are a number of different coding systems. Notice that it is not a method of recording the content of the discussion, i.e. what was said – interaction-process analysis describes the style of behaviour only.

Many of the coding systems which have been devised are complex and difficult to use without practice, but you might like to try the codes devised for use by students in the Open University Social Studies foundation course, D101, listed by Bell on page 113.

As Bell warns, even with a simple classification like this it may be difficult to disentangle the different categories: a single sentence may contain several behaviour styles – proposing and disagreeing, for instance.

Bell also has some useful suggestions for recording behaviour during a meeting, using for example the D101 categories (the table plan illustrated in Figure 10.1, on page 114) and also for summarising the results of your observation (the grid in Figure 10.2 on page 115). Remember that it will not be enough simply to record what happened: you will also need to offer some analysis and interpretation, i.e. say what you think it means and why.

Analysing content and interventions

If your interest in observing is to find out the content of a discussion, i.e. what was said (and possibly also who said what) then your task is rather simpler, though again you will need to devise some categories and decide where a particular statement fits into your plan.

Here again Bell gives some useful examples of recording methods, which you can adapt according to your own area of interest.

If you simply want to record which topics received most discussion, you could use a chart which has only two dimensions, topics discussed and time spent, with a column to record the percentage of time spent on each topic. If you have access to an agenda for the meeting, it will obviously be a help in drawing up your categories – or you could choose categories to suit the aspects of the meeting which you want to focus on.

If your main interest is in who made most contributions and spent most time speaking, however, you might draw up a chart like the one shown in Figure 10.3 (page 116). In this recording system, the members of the group are listed in a column at the left (so again you would need to have this information in advance). A vertical line opposite the name is used to indicate that that person spoke for a set time (say half a minute) or less. A horizontal line following the vertical one means that the same person continued to speak for the same set period. As you can see from the example in Figure 10.3, the results of a chart like this will allow you to see clearly who did most of the talking, and who was silent.

If you want to include both sorts of information – i.e. who spoke most, *and* on what topics – you will need a more complex system, which may be difficult to manage in chart form. Bell suggests that it may be best to make fuller notes during the course of the meeting and then to transfer the information to a summary chart.

Shaw (1978: 10) suggests using sheets of lined paper, with each line representing one minute, to record events in the meeting itself. Methods like these can provide quite detailed information for analysis, and from your memory of the meeting you will be able to fill in details which the chart cannot show.

<table>
<tr><td>Activity 3</td><td>Just to check your understanding of observation methods, take a careful look at the chart in figure 10.2 on page 115. What sort of information does it give you about the roles taken by participants in the meeting? Are there any inferences you can draw from this information alone?</td></tr>
</table>

One thing that struck me was that the interventions made by different members were relatively balanced. Judith seems to have been the most active member (and, along with Fred and Sandy, the most prone to disagree) and Brendan and Stephen the least active, but there is not a wide gap (four entries to two). It's also possible to identify, tentatively, different styles of participation – for instance, the chairperson's three entries are all in the 'proposing' category, while Ian's style seems to be to provide information or clarification and to 'build' on the proposals made by others.

Recording interactions

If your interest is in who talks to whom, you will need to prepare a seat plan, like the one in figure 10.1, beforehand and write in the names of group members when they sit down. Arrows can then be used to show who talks to whom, and additional arrow heads can record the number of interactions between particular individuals. Ticks next to names can be used to show communication to the whole group, while ticks next to 'M' can indicate multiple speaking.

Once again, a chart like this makes it easy to pick out the pattern of interactions in the group. You can see obvious pairings or groupings and begin to ask yourself questions about the significance of what you observe.

Recording physical behaviour

All of the examples Bell uses, apart from video recording, assume that you will be recording something like a meeting or a classroom discussion, and that your interest will be in what is said, how, and by whom.

But you might have chosen a topic for which you need to observe people's physical behaviour – for instance, the way they move about in a public place. In this case, you will again need to decide what aspects of the behaviour you are focusing on, what categories to use and how often to record. But you will also need to make decisions concerning, for instance, the position from which you will observe the behaviour, whether or not you need to ask for permission, and whether you can record during the observation (and if so, how).

Below I have reprinted an activity from an NEC course for zoo keepers, *Zoo Animal Management*, which may give you some ideas about recording the physical behaviour of people (or animals).

A good example of a personal record was published in the *International Zoo Year Book*. It shows the movements of an elephant during each hour interval after her release (a) when public feeding was allowed (b) after the prohibition of public feeding (Fig. 1).

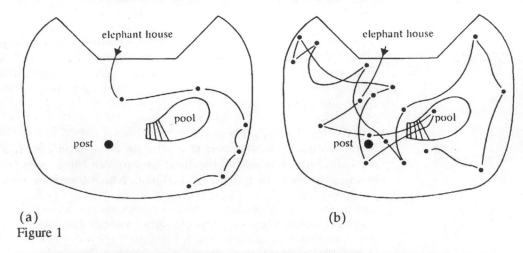

(a)   (b)

Figure 1

Record the movements of an animal of your choice each two minutes for one hour. Start by sketching a plan of the enclosure and marking any features, as in Figure 1 above. Put a dot to mark the position of the animal at the end of two minutes and join up the dots. It will be easiest and most fun if you choose a moderately active animal – not a speed demon or one that's asleep!

3 Selecting a method

These methods of recording what you observe may seem straightforward, but there will inevitably be problems in deciding which categories of behaviour to use, and also whether behaviour fits a given category. It is particularly difficult, because you have to be able to identify categories on the spot and record them quickly. You will need to get all the practice you can before you have to record your group, meeting or class for real.

Observing a small group for a few minutes may present relatively few problems, but the larger the group, and the longer the observation goes on, the more complicated your recording becomes. This is not to say that you should not attempt observation studies, but it is probably a good idea to limit the aspects of behaviour which you intend to record.

There are many educational and social studies which use observation methods, and which provide examples of charts, grids, categories and methods of recording which will give you a range of useful ideas for devising schemes of your own. I have listed a number of the most useful ones at the end of this unit, and it would be a good idea for you to look at several examples from the list, and try out the methods they suggest, before you make up your mind about recording methods. However, as Bell warns on page 117, you will inevitably have to adapt the method to your own needs, devise your own categories and symbols, and decide how often you need to record.

Activity 4	Begin by reading the section 'Selecting a Method' on pages 116–117 of Bell.

Spend some time if you can looking at some of the studies listed in the Suggested reading list and the end of this unit and getting some ideas of ways in which you might record your observations.

Then take every opportunity you can of trying out your ideas. If you have to attend a meeting, try out different methods of recording under certain headings or categories. If there is a meeting or discussion on television or on the radio, put yourself into the role of non-participant observer. Decide what you will be looking for, and start making notes. In this way, you will be able to get some idea of how difficult or straightforward different approaches are.

You should end up with some firm ideas about what method works for you, which you can use when you do your observation for your study.

4 Preparing for the observation

As Bell reminds us, preparation is all-important. You may only have a limited opportunity for observation – perhaps only one meeting or class.

Before you go in to observe, you need to have prepared whatever recording sheets you are going to use, discussed with the person responsible for the group or meeting how you will be introduced and where you will sit, and practised observing similar groups as often as you have the opportunity.

Reading	Read the section 'Preparation' in Chapter 10 in Bell (pages 117–118).

Activity 5	The time has come to put your methods into practice. Conduct the observation you planned, taking notes in the session and filling in the details as soon as possible afterwards.

You now need to think about what you have learned from your observations, as the next section in Bell explains. What were the 'significant events', and how should they be interpreted?

5 Afterwards: analysing what went on

Reading

Read the final section in Chapter 10 in Bell, 'After the Event' (pages 118–119), now. What questions does your observation suggest, or answer? How can you place what you have observed in a wider context?

6 Checklist

Use the 'Observation Studies Checklist' on pages 119–120 of Bell to guide you if you plan to include observation methods as part of your research.

Assignment 4

When you have completed the work for Units 6–10, you will have developed a research tool which can be used for data collection. Before you go on to Part 3, you have an opportunity to get some feedback on the research instrument you have designed, and on your data collection so far.

Depending on your choice of research method, send your tutor:

* sample records from your library research, and a note of the bibliographical system you plan to use

plus one or more of the following, if you are using any of the methods described in Units 7 to 10:

* a sample questionnaire
* an interview schedule or checklist of topics to be covered
* instructions and questions or a recording form (if used) for diary or critical incident methods
* charts, grids or checklists for use in recording observations.

You are extremely unlikely to have used all these methods, but, if your research topic is a complex one like the example used in Bell, you may well have two or three.

Together with the questionnaire, schedule, checklist etc., write a note for your tutor giving some information on how the research tool for each method you plan to use was devised and tested, and your plans for using it. Describe any difficulties you had in designing your research instrument(s), and add any queries you have on methodology.

If your original schedule has had to be altered, explain what happened and when you now expect to complete the stages of data collection and writing up. Ask for help if you need it!

If your schedule allows, wait for a response from your tutor before starting the main part of your data collection.

7 Suggested reading

When you did your initial reading and literature review (Unit 4) I asked you to take note of the methods used by researchers working in your topic area. These can give you some good ideas about planning, recording and analysing your data.

There are many examples of observation studies in educational and social research. Bell gives a list at the end of Chapter 10. A number which provide useful guidance on recording are: Simon and Boyer (1975), Flanders (1970), Wragg and Kerry (1978), Galton (1978), Cohen (1976), Williams (1984) and Hopkins (1985) – you'll find the publication details for these in Bell's References section.

I am obviously not suggesting that you should try to read all of these studies, and the older ones in particular may be difficult to locate. But if you are planning to observe what goes on in a classroom, I recommend the Rediguide by Wragg and Kerry. Chapter 13 in Bell *et al.* (1984), 'Observing and Recording Meetings' by G. L. Williams, is equally useful if you intend to record meetings, as either a participant or non-participant observer. Hopkins is aimed particularly at the teacher observing in the classroom, but his guidelines can be applied to other situations as well.

Finally, Chapter 5, 'Case Studies', in Cohen and Manion (1989) provides helpful additional information about observation, including six educational case studies, chosen to illustrate different styles of research, which may give you ideas for your own investigation.

96

PART 3: ANALYSING AND PRESENTING YOUR DATA

Unit 11:   Collecting and analysing your data

Unit 12:   Writing the report   Assignment 5

Introduction

By this stage in the course, you should have finalised your plan of campaign, and agreed it with your tutor; chosen and piloted your research instruments (questionnaires, interviews, diaries, observation schedules, etc.); and taken note of your tutor's comments on them following Assignment 4.

You are now ready to move into the final, important stage: collecting, recording and analysing your evidence, and writing up the final report of your research. If you are up to date with preparation, have piloted your methods and considered how your information will be analysed, the actual stage of information gathering should be straightforward.

Before you get started, though, here are one or two pieces of advice for you to consider.

I have already stressed how important it is to think about how the data you collect will be analysed: in Part 2 you were asked to look ahead at Unit 11, and at Chapter 11 in Bell, for guidance on this.

I have also made the point that data mean very little until they have been analysed and related to your initial questions or hypothesis. This means that you always need to keep in mind what you intend to do with the data you collect: collecting mountains of data without any plan is not a good idea!

You also need to keep in mind the way in which you will present your findings and write the report, while information is being gathered. The golden rule is to write up everything as you go along, even though you will almost certainly need to make many changes to these early drafts.

There may be limitations, too, that you need to keep in mind.

If you do not have a background in statistics, it is probably not a good idea to use a form of analysis that requires advanced statistical techniques, particularly if your research involves small numbers which are unlikely to produce statistically significant results anyway. However, simple statistical techniques are useful for analysing and presenting information clearly, and this is covered in Unit 11. And if you do want to tackle more complex and sophisticated statistical analysis of your data, you will find some Suggested reading at the end of Unit 11.

'Keep it simple' is good advice for researchers as well as programmers. A worthwhile and even valuable study can be carried out using a straightforward design and simple methods of analysis. Unit 11 again shows you how to do this, in particular for the information arising from small-scale surveys using questionnaires or structured interviews.

The other limitation to be aware of is the extent to which you will be justified in making generalisations from your data, which is almost certain to be relatively limited in scope.

Reading

Bell has some comments to make on this, and on the other advice I have given above, in the Introduction to Part 3 of her book (page 125–126). I suggest you look at this now.

About Part 3

As you can see from page 97 this part of the course has two units, and one assignment.

You should already have had a look at the work for Unit 11, on collecting and analysing your data, when you were designing your research instruments for studies involving people (Units 7 to 10). Unit 12 covers the elements which you should include in your final report, and the stages of writing up the report itself: outlining, drafting, editing, and preparing references. The final assignment asks you to send a draft of the final report of your investigation to your tutor.

What to do if things go wrong

In an ideal world, there are no hitches, researchers have no family or professional crises, and all data are collected within the planned schedule. Life is not always like that.

In the Postscript to *Doing Your Research Project*, Bell has some valuable advice which I think you need to be aware of right now.

Reading

Read the first paragraph on page 165 in Bell carefully now, and take its message to heart!

Finally, remember that in most cases your time will be very limited, and that this will limit what you can reasonably hope to accomplish. The purpose of this course is not to require you to produce work which would warrant a PhD – though some of you may be doing just that. It is intended, as I said in my Introduction, to give you an opportunity to actually do some research, and, by doing it, to become familiar with some of the techniques which will allow you to adopt systematic and effective methods of enquiry now and in the future.

By working systematically through this course, you will have acquired the tools of the trade. I hope these will stand you in good stead throughout your life as a researcher.

Unit 11: Collecting and analysing your data

1 Introduction

Having designed and tested your data-collection instruments in Part 2, the time has come to try them out in earnest. Assignment 4, and your tutor's comments on it, should have provided you with a good foundation for the main body of your research.

Check with your schedule regularly as you go along, to make sure that you are not spending more time on data collection than you can afford. If you have to cut short the information gathering stage to meet your deadline, speak to your tutor and see if you can agree on an adjustment to your original plan. The main thing is not to let the project get out of hand.

This unit is about how to interpret, organise and present the information you collect from your research. It covers:

- recording and presenting the information you might get from several of the question types discussed in Unit/Chapter 7

- straightforward methods of collecting and recording data from questionnaires and interviews, using summary sheets to draw the results together for analysis

- the use of different kinds of tables, charts and graphs to present results diagrammatically

- simple methods of analysing data.

It is based on Chapter 11 in Bell. The sort of investigation Bell has in mind is a small-scale survey, based on questionnaires or structured interviews, although many of the points will apply equally to the other methods of gathering information from people which we discussed in Part 2 of the course. Bell covers all the points listed above in the course of the chapter, but I have separated them out so that we can focus on each area in turn.

Tools for analysis

As you discovered in Part 2, even before you begin to collect your own data, you need to be aware of the ways in which you can analyse and present the information you collect. You also need to be able to understand the ways in which statistical information may be presented in your sources. For both of these reasons, you need some knowledge of statistics.

However, you don't need any special statistical knowledge to understand and use the methods Bell describes. The chapter is based on her conviction that 'it is perfectly possible to produce a sound project without much knowledge of statistics' (Letter to NEC, 31 March 1993). If your research is qualitative, you may not need even these basic tools, though you should read through the chapter in any case to see if it gives you any new ideas on how you could manage and present your data. If you want or need to explore more sophisticated forms of statistical analysis, you will find suggestions for further reading at the end of this unit, and the Bell chapter.

Bell has not included computer analysis of data, mostly because the techniques she describes are simple enough to be done easily by hand. In this unit, I also haven't discussed the use of computers and computer packages for statistical analysis. You are simply not likely to need to use a computer for analysing relatively small amounts of data. A calculator, and some simple geometric tools – a ruler, plus a compass and protractor if you are drawing pie charts – are all you will need to do any of the analyses or reproduce any of the diagrams described below. However, if you have access to a microcomputer with a program for drawing graphs and charts (often included in spreadsheet programs) you will find that this makes presenting your information in graphical form very easy – so easy, in fact, that you may be tempted to over-use the technique! Similarly, if your computer has a database program, this can be used for collecting and summarising information, and presenting it in the form of tables. None of these tools is necessary, however: pen, paper and ruler will do just as well.

2 Question types revisited

Bell begins her chapter with a reminder of the seven question types identified by Michael Youngman, which were first described in Chapter 7. In Chapter 11, she uses four of these question types to illustrate different ways of interpreting and presenting the answers you might get.

Activity 1

How many of Youngman's question types can you recall? Try to remember, then look back at Chapter 7 (pages 76–77) to check your memory and remind yourself of the main features of each type.

List questions

As the name suggests, list questions provide a list of possible answers and ask the respondent to choose one or more.

Reading

Begin by reading the introduction to Chapter 11, 'Interpretation and Presentation of the Evidence', and the section headed 'List Questions' (pages 127 – 130). Skim over the information on preparing a summary sheet and the use of tables and graphs for the moment, and focus on the sample question itself (Question 1, page 128).

- If you were answering this question, would you be clear what to do?
- Does your research instrument (e.g. questionnaire or interview schedule) contain any questions of this type?
- Can you foresee any problems in analysing the response to this type of question?

I think the question wording itself is clear, and would probably provide the information about qualifications which the researcher is seeking. Perhaps deliberately, there's no mention of technical or vocational qualifications – students would have to write them in as 'Other'. The only analysis problems I can foresee are that you would need to find a way of recording the answers which would allow you to note multiple responses; and you would need to decide how (or whether) to code the 'Other' responses.

Category questions

Category questions ask respondents to place themselves in one of a selection of categories; as Bell warns in Chapter 7, the categories should be exclusive, so that only one answer is possible.

Reading

Now read the section in Chapter 11 on category questions (pages 130–138). Again, focus on the wording of the sample question (in two versions) and skim rapidly over the information on statistical analysis and graph presentation – we will come back to this.

- Do you have any questions like this in your research instrument?
- Which version of Question 2 seems more successful to you? Why?

Both versions of Question 2 can be described as category questions (since everybody belongs in one, and only one, age category) but the alternative on page 133 is more typical of this type. Alternative Question 2 will be quicker to answer and easier to analyse, especially if replies are coded as in the example. People may also be more willing to place themselves in an age band than to reveal their exact age. However, the information is of course less precise: you would have to decide whether that mattered. The main point about a category question is that, as in the example, the categories should be distinct, without gaps or overlapping.

Grid questions

A grid question is a way of asking several questions at the same time, and allows you to make more complex comparisons than a simple list question. But because of the greater complexity, they need care in wording, and in analysing.

Reading

Read the section 'Grids' (pages 138–139) focusing on the sample question (Question 3). Compare it with Question 1 and notice how the information you would get from Question 3 is more detailed and precise.

How many questions are combined here?

I make it five questions, each with four possible responses. If you have a question like this in your survey, you will need to remember to record the answers to each question separately for each respondent.

Scale questions

Scale questions ask respondents to rate their attitude to some question along a scale, e.g. from 1 to 5.

Reading

Bell introduces scale questions on pages 139–141, and gives an example of a simple scale question, using the so-called Likert scale, on page 140 (Question 4). She suggests that additional information, on the students' faculty, could be sought by asking students to complete a 'combined Likert scale/grid question', which might produce results like the ones shown in Table 11.4.

Try and imagine what this combined question might look like. How many different responses would need to be recorded for each respondent?

I imagine this could be a grid with the faculties down the left side (where the qualifications were in Question 3) and the scale numbers across the top, rather like the layout of Table 11.4 itself. A single tick would identify both the faculty and the level of optimism for each respondent, which would make analysis easier than a separate question asking students to identify their faculty. Unlike the grid in Question 3, though, you should only get one answer for each respondent.

Verbal questions

Reading

Bell deals briefly with analysing the information from open, or verbal, questions on page 147: please read this now. The problems are similar to those you would face in analysing any documentary source; Chapters 6 and 7 give additional guidelines on this.

3 Recording the information you collect

We are now going to look at possible ways of recording information from your data collection, using examples based on the first two question types (list and category questions) that Bell uses.

Using summary sheets to record your data

It is important, as we have already said, to plan the way in which you are going to analyse your data at the same time as you prepare your questionnaire or interview schedule. One way of making analysis easy is to prepare summary sheets on which you can record responses to your questionnaire or interview questions. If you design the summary sheet at the same time as the questions, as I suggested in Unit 7, it may also suggest ways in which your questionnaire or schedule could be simplified.

Activity 2

A simple summary sheet for Question 1 is shown on page 129 of Bell, and a more sophisticated version, with instructions for completing it, is on pages 137–38. Read these sections again now and note down the main steps you will need to go through when recording your data.

My summary of the procedures you will need to go through if you follow Bell's advice (here, and in Chapter 7) looks like this:

1 If possible, use a coding frame on your questionnaire or interview schedule to make it easier to record responses (e.g. 1 = 'Yes', 2 = 'No').

2 Prepare a summary sheet like the one on page 137 which will allow you to record the responses from each questionnaire or interview.

3 Number questionnaires or schedules when completed, for reference purposes. If the responses are not anonymous, the numbering system can be used to categorise different groups of respondents.

4 Check returned questionnaires for completeness, and return any which have gaps, if it is possible to identify the respondent.

5 Decide what to do about verbal questions:

– devise a coding frame after all responses are in or

– copy replies onto separate sheets, read through to look for patterns, and use selected replies as quotations in the report.

6 Code responses
(if they are not pre-coded like those for Alternative Question 2).

7 Transfer the responses from the questionnaires or schedules to the summary sheet, using ticks or tallies.

8 Add up the totals for each question and use them as the basis for your analysis (see Sections 4 and 5 for suggestions on this).

9 Keep the original questionnaires safely until the research is completed, in case there is a query and you need to refer to them.

If your research plan includes any form of data-collecting instrument which would benefit from a summary sheet like the one described, work out how this sheet will be arranged, and what coding system you plan to use, at the same time as you design your questionnaire, interview schedule, observation checklists or charts, etc.

You might find it useful to rule vertical columns for each answer code within a question, and to draw a horizontal line after each entry, to make certain that you can identify exactly where each response belongs. Or you could use squared paper to record your results.

If you have access to a microcomputer with a database program, you could use it to analyse your results (and to present them in tables) but even so you might find it easier to collect the responses manually first, using a system like the one described by Bell.

4 Analysing and presenting your information

Once the data has been collected, and summarised using a method similar to the one described above, it needs to be analysed. How you decide to do this will depend on a number of factors, including your thesis (or what you are trying to prove). But using the fictional data from the four questions in Chapter 11, Bell gives some examples which illustrate the different ways in which this information could be analysed and presented to the reader. They should give you some ideas as to how you could present the information from your own study, as well as explaining how to go about it.

Remember the old saying: 'a picture is worth a thousand words'. A table or diagram is usually a more effective way of presenting a set of data than pages of written description.

Tables

A table is one of the simplest ways of presenting statistical information, like the results from a survey. It can involve just a set of headings or categories with totals for each, as in Tables 11.1, 11.2 and 11.3, or be used to set out more complex data like that in Table 11.4.

Any time you have a stack of figures or details which can be sorted into categories, it is worth thinking about using a table to summarise it clearly. To test for yourself the difference between a table and ordinary text, try writing out the results from Table 11.1 (or, if you want an even better demonstration, Table 11.4) as continuous prose, e.g. 'Six of the students surveyed had no qualifications, while 28 had obtained 'O' level or GCSE passes...'. Compare your sentences with the table and see which you find gives you the clearer overall picture.

Another advantage is that, once your readers have the table before them and can take in the total picture at a glance, you can refer them to particular details that you want to emphasise (as Bell does in the last paragraph on page 129).

Look through your research notes, and the information you are starting to collect. Would any of it be clearer in tabular form?

If so, and if you are typing or wordprocessing your report yourself, check that you know how to use the tab feature on your machine, or, if you have the facilities, how to set up a database (for tables involving words and figures) or spreadsheet (for tables mostly of figures, or ones which need totals or other calculations) report.

Percentages

One simple way of making your figures more meaningful is to convert them to **percentages**. We can illustrate this by looking at how the information from Questions 1 and 2 might look in the form of percentages.

Advertisers may go for phrases like 'nine out of ten cats prefer...' but, as with tables, most people find it easier to visualise information which is presented as, say, '97%' rather than 'five hundred and eighty-two out of six hundred'.

Activity 5

Bell gives percentage values, in the text, for most of the results from the sample Question 1 (on qualifications). Check that you know how to calculate a percentage by working out what percentage of the sample had 'O' levels or GCSEs before entry.

Because there are fifty students in the sample, calculating the percentage is easy. As the percentage represents the number out of 100, you just double the number out of 50 (28 in this case) to get the result (56%). The general rule is to divide the result by the total number in the sample (28 divided by 50) which will give you a decimal. Multiply this by 100 to get the percentage.

Reading

Percentage results, as well as numbers, are given in the pie chart on page 136 (Figure 11.3) which summarises the replies to Question 2. Compare this with the numerical results for the same question, in Table 11.2 and Figure 11.2, and see which you think is clearer.

Notice that here in Figure 11.3, and again in Figure 11.6 on page 142, Bell gives the actual numbers as well as the percentages. This is particularly important for Figure 11.6 – see if you can work out why (I'll come back to this). But it's good practice in general when dealing with relatively small numbers, to avoid giving a misleading impression of the scale of the survey.

It might be clearer to present your information graphically, perhaps as a bar chart, rather than simply in table or percentage form. Bell gives guidance on this too.

Bar charts, plain and fancy

Chapter 11 shows several different ways of presenting the answers from the sample questions as bar charts of various sorts.

Figure 11.1 on page 130 is a simple **vertical bar chart** showing the qualifications held by students (as summarised in Table 11.1 on page 129).

The next table and bar chart (Table 11.2 and Figure 11.2) show two different ways of presenting the data from Question 2, about student age. Figure 11.2 is a type of bar chart called a **histogram**: notice that the bars are touching, because the variable, age, is continuous. Figure 11.4 at the top of page 139 is a **compound bar chart**. Figure 11.6 on page 142 summarises the information in Table 11.4 as a **percentage component bar chart**. Notice that Figure 11.6 is also a **horizontal bar chart**. You might also like to compare this with the simpler way of presenting information from the original Question 4, in Table 11.5 and Figure 11.5.

Reading

Look carefully at the different types of bar charts Bell illustrates. See which method you think is clearest. Does your answer vary depending on the type of information which is being presented?

When deciding how to present your own data, you will have to make a judgement as to which method will make the point you wish to illustrate most clearly.

As Bell points out, the different charts she illustrates have different purposes. For example, Figure 11.4, the compound bar chart, uses three bars with different shading to indicate both what sort of qualifications students have and how many years they have studied to obtain them. It's worth noticing what this chart does not show, as well. Students with no experience of study since 18, and those with 'other' qualifications, do not appear on this chart (though they are included in Question 3). And notice that it isn't possible to identify the study experience of individual students from the chart – only of the total sample. So, although a student may have spent three years on 'A' level study, and a further two years on an Access course, there is no way of identifying this from the graph. The totals have a different meaning from those in some of the other examples: it is the cumulative experience of the student group, and not the experience of individual students, which is being shown. Once again, it is a matter of knowing what you wish to show, and designing your presentation with that in mind.

You may need to show several different views of the same information. For example, Figure 11.5 shows the general student view of exam prospects, while Figure 11.6 shows how different sub-groups of students vary in their expectations. Both might give useful information.

Sometimes, it is possible to combine these different views on the same graph or chart. A **percentage component bar chart** like the one in Figure 11.6 can be used to illustrate both the expectations of exam results within each faculty, and the varying optimism in different faculties. Here, what the bars do not show, unless you look at the figures as well as the percentage labels, is the relative number of students in each faculty sample. Each bar represents 100% of the students in that faculty, and the bars are therefore the same length whether the numbers are 4 (maths) or 16 (social science).

When constructing charts like these, the important things to remember is that the scales should start from zero, and that the heights or lengths of the bars should be proportional to the numbers they represent.

Bar charts are easy to draw by hand, using graph paper and a ruler, but, as I said earlier, if you are able to use a spreadsheet program which produces graphs, or a stand-alone graphing program on a microcomputer, you will be able to get an even more professional result.

Pie charts

Another popular way of presenting this type of information is the **pie chart**. Figure 11.3 shows how the information from Question 2 would appear in the form of a pie chart. The chart shows the percentage of students in each age band.

Notice that the pie chart can also be used to show the relative sizes of the different age groups as a percentage of the total, rather more clearly than the bar chart in Figure 11.2.

The instructions at the bottom of page 135 explain what you will need to do if you are to calculate and draw pie charts (without a computer program, that is).

Activity 6

Once more, look back at the examples of different ways of presenting the information from Questions 1 to 4: table, percentages, simple or compound bar chart, percentage component bar chart, pie chart.

Which method of presenting this information seems clearest to you? Which, if any, look appropriate for your own research?

It goes without saying that, however you present your information, it should be as accurate as possible, and this requires careful checking.

5 Some simple statistical measures

In Chapter 11, Bell illustrates several simple methods of analysing data, using the information from Question 2 and from some imaginary coursework and exam scores. They are:

- Averages: mode, median and mean
- Measures of dispersion
- Scattergrams

These are slightly more complicated to calculate than the methods we have looked at so far, and you may decide that your research does not need anything so elaborate.

But it is worth reading what Bell has to say about these methods – and you may find that some of them are useful ways of summarising some aspect of your research findings.

Averages: mode, median, mean

One of the difficulties with statistics is that the terms used make things sound more complicated than they really are.

Reading

Read the sections in Bell which deal with averages (pages 131 and 133–134) and check that you understand what is meant by the following terms:
- arithmetic mean
- median
- mode
- measure of central tendency
- class interval.

As well as the age distribution, we might want to know the average age of the student sample. As Bell explains, there are three different types of **average** (known in statistics as **measures of central tendency**) and we would need to decide which of these is the most appropriate.

Bell begins by describing the three sorts of average: the **mode**, the **median** and the **mean**. She describes how to calculate each, and then goes on to discuss how to decide which should be used when.

Check that you understand:
- how the mode, median and mean are defined
- how they are calculated
- when to use them.

The *arithmetic mean*, or simply the mean, is what we usually think of as an average. Generally speaking it is simple to calculate. But when the data are grouped, as in the age categories for Question 2, calculating the mean is a bit more complicated, because we need to take into account the number of people in each age group or class, and the 'average age' which a group like 20-29 represents. We do this by multiplying the number in each class, or class frequency, by the middle number or mid-point of each class or age group. We can then calculate the mean or average in the usual way, by adding up the results of multiplying the frequency times the midpoint for each class, and then dividing the sum by the total number in the sample, which is 50.

The table at the top of page 134 shows how this works. The first column shows the age groups or classes, the second shows the frequency or numbers in each class (with the total number, 50, at the bottom) the third column shows the mid-point or half-way point for each class, and the fourth column shows the result of multiplying the frequency by the mid-point, again with the total at the bottom. If you are not mathematically confident, work through it slowly, using the explanation below the table to guide you, and check that you can understand how the calculation works.

Which average?

As Bell explains, in practice you would use only one sort of average to analyse your data. And you would decide which average to use by looking at the shape and spread of the distribution. The spread, or dispersion, can also be calculated using another set of statistical procedures.

Measures of dispersion

Measures of dispersion allow us to measure the variability within a set of data. Another way of describing this is to say that they allow us to describe how the data is dispersed or 'spread out'.

Bell describes these measures briefly on pages 132-33. She also explains how measures of dispersion such as the **range** and the **interquartile range** (but not the **standard deviation**) are calculated. If you need to know about such things, there are plenty of books, including those in the Suggested Reading list at the end of this unit, to help you.

Correlations and scattergrams

Scattergrams are a way of determining whether or not there is a relationship, or **correlation**, between two pieces of information. The example Bell uses is the relationship between coursework scores and exam scores, where one would generally expect some sort of positive relationship.

Reading

Bell, Chapter 11, pages 143–146, describes how to draw scattergrams or scattergraphs and what they will look like for data with a perfect positive, perfect negative, or positive but not perfect correlation.

Check that you understand how this works. Is it likely to be useful to you in analysing your results?

Activity 7

Work out which, if any, of the above methods of analysing and presenting data will be useful to you in your project report.

Look at the suggestions for further reading if you need more detailed information.

6 Conclusion

This unit and the chapter in Bell are only a brief introduction to the world of graphs and statistics. They illustrate some ways of analysing data which you may find useful in presenting the information collected as a result of your investigation, but there are plenty of other ways, and you may find ways of setting out the information you have which will be different but equally clear.

If you are interested in knowing more about statistical analysis, there are some useful sources in the booklists below and on pages 149–150 of Bell.

7 Checklist

Use the Analysis and Presentation of Information Checklist on pages 148–149 of Bell to summarise the information contained in this unit.

8 Suggested reading

A very useful source of guidance on statistical methods is Hugh Coolican (1990) *Research Methods and Statistics in Psychology*, London, Hodder and Stoughton. As the title suggests, it is aimed particularly at psychology students, but there are useful chapters on methodology, including sampling methods, the use of experiments, observational methods, questionnaires and interviews, which would be valuable for anyone undertaking social research. Part III, 'Dealing with data', covers the measurement scales introduced in this unit, descriptive and inferential statistics, probability, and tests using qualitative data. There is also a valuable section on ethics, and an Appendix on planning practicals and writing reports.

Other suggestions are listed at the end of Chapter 11 of Bell, some with her recommendations. Also worth mentioning is M. B. Youngman (1984) *Foundation Statistics for Education: Part I Principles* (January); *Part II Procedures* (March), University of Nottingham School of Education.

Unit 12: Writing the report

1   **Getting started**

2   **Guidelines for preparing a report**

3   **Stages of writing your report**   Assignment 5

4   **A final word**

5   **Checklists**

6   **Suggested reading**

1 Getting started

You are now in the final stages of your investigation. I am assuming that you have completed your research, and recorded your findings using the guidelines in Part 1 (especially Units 3 and 4) and in Unit 11.

But, as Bell reminds us in the introduction to her Chapter 12, 'Writing the Report', even when all the hard work of gathering and analysing the evidence is complete, there is still another big job to be done – writing the report.

However, if you have been following the advice in Bell and in the course so far, and have done all the activities and assignments related to your chosen research methods, it will be a job that you have already begun to work on. As has been said several times already, you should begin to write parts of the report throughout the planning, reading and information-gathering process. If you have written up sections as soon as they were ready, you will have first drafts of parts of the report available now, before you start the important task of pulling everything together.

Look at what you have done already

Before we go on to look at the shape of the ideal report, and at the stages of writing up, take time to remind yourself of how much you have accomplished.

Activity 1

Stop and think about the work that you have done already which will contribute to the writing of your report. You might like to make a list of the elements or 'raw ingredients' of the report that you have available, and compare it with my suggestions below.

Here are some of the things that might be on your list:

1   *Clear objectives*

    If you followed the guidelines in Unit 2 of this course, you will not have started your project until you had drafted clear objectives, although you may have needed to revise them as your investigation developed.

2   *An outline of major headings or sections*

    As I suggested in Unit 3, you may have an outline of major sections of the report already on cards, with topics grouped within these sections. This should make the job of structuring your report much easier. It is not too late to do this now – look back at Unit 3 for a reminder of how you might go about it.

3   *Bibliographical   references*

In Unit 3, you also learned to record the details of all the sources you consulted, either on cards or in some other way that suited you. You should therefore have your bibliographical cards in good order, with notes and useful quotations to guide your writing.

4   *An evaluation of your reading*

If you completed the work for Unit 4, you will already have produced an evaluation of what you have read about your topic.

5   *Draft sections*

Finally, you should also have sections of your report available in draft, having written them up as you finished each stage of the research.

If you have all of these resources to hand, congratulations! The actual job of writing up should be comparatively straightforward.

The first task is to gather together all your resource materials, and sort them into an order which will make the job of writing easier.

Activity 2

Gather together:

- the notes from your reading
- the project outline and literature review you prepared for Assignments 2 and 3
- the sample research instruments and explanation of your research plan you prepared for Assignment 4
- summary sheets from your data collection
- any drafts you have already prepared as you completed sections of your research.

If you have been working through the course and completing the assignments as you go, you should have quite a lot of valuable material to hand.

Sort your notes and drafts into the sections you plan for the report, and put them in rough order. These are the raw materials for your write-up, and hopefully you will discover that quite a lot of the basic spadework has been done already, and that you have at least the skeleton of your finished report.

Look through your drafts and notes and try to work out what you will need to do to convert them into a finished report.

Your first drafts will almost certainly need to be revised, or even completely rewritten, but hopefully you will have the foundations in place already.

Check Section 2, ' Guidelines for preparing a report', below, before you make a final decision about the sections into which you will divide your report.

Develop a writing plan

As well as the materials from your research, you will need a certain amount of discipline to carry you through the writing stage and make certain that the report is completed, and completed on time if you are working to a deadline.

Everybody has different ways of working, but Bell gives some useful advice in Chapter 12, which I hope will give you some ideas for working out a writing plan that suits you.

Reading

Read the first section of Chapter 12 in Bell, 'Getting Started' (pages 151–153).

Use the guidelines on pages 152–153 of Bell to draw up your own writing plan, based on what you know about the way you work. Try to work out when you work best (morning? late at night?) and also when you will be able to find time for writing. It's a good idea to draw up a detailed schedule, or mark off time in your diary, to remind you of your plans and when your deadlines are.

2 Guidelines for preparing a report

If you are writing your report as part of a course of study, there are certain conventions that you may need to follow. In this section, we use Bell to take you through the stages involved in structuring an academic report, and outline major features which are common to most reports. There are, however, no universal rules which insist on one structure rather than another. You will need to check particular points, such as length, and any other special requirements, with your own institution. Most institutions issue guidelines explaining how a report for a particular award should be structured and presented, and you will obviously need to follow these carefully.

Even if you are not writing your report for academic credit, you might find it useful to follow similar guidelines for structuring your report, or at least to skim through this section to get some ideas about conventions of report-writing.

There are many books which have been published on the skills and techniques of actually writing a report. If you are not confident of your skills as a writer, you might like to look at one or more of the texts listed in the Suggested reading section at the end of this unit, for more detailed guidance and advice.

Structure of an academic report

Read the section 'Structuring the Report' in Bell (pages 153–159), which outlines the major sections and features which that a report or dissertation will usually contain. Look at each of these sections in turn, to make clear what they might contain and how you might approach the task of writing them. Take notes as you go of anything that looks useful.

In my notes, I have divided the information Bell gives into two categories. The first list takes you through the sections which your report is likely to contain, and suggests the sort of information which belongs in each. The second list, under the heading 'features of an academic report', itemises the 'nuts and bolts' as Bell calls them – things like tables, quotations, the layout of the title page.

My headings are mostly the same as Bell's, but there are a few variations. Your institution may have cut and dried guidelines for what your report should contain and how it should appear, but the general rule is to consider what your readers will need to know, and how it can be presented most clearly.

1   *Outline of the research*

The aim of the outline is to give a clear picture of the aims, methods and results of the research. Only the essential points should be included at this stage. The outline may be replaced by an abstract (9 below) or combined with the aims and purposes (3 below).

You should find at least a starting point in the outline you were asked to prepare for Assignment 2, but if your research plan has changed substantially, it will need to be rewritten.

It is a good idea to write this section (and other summary sections like the abstract, and of course the conclusions) last. You should also try to write Sections 4, 5 and 6 (in my list) in order, and without a break if you can.

2   *Review of the literature*

You should have a draft review in the work you did for Unit 4, as part of Assignment 3. It may need to be revised, to take account of additional reading or to tighten up the structure, but you should not need to start from the beginning.

Remember the warning that only books and articles which relate directly to the topic should be included. Look back again at Woodley's (1985) review of the literature relating to mature students if you need a model.

3   *Aims and purpose of the study*

This is where you tell the reader what the research is for: the problem you are hoping to tackle and how you hope your research will contribute. You should have a draft of this in the statement of objectives or hypothesis you prepared early on, but it will need rewording in the light of your research. Another good section to leave until the end!

4   *Methodology*

This section is about what you did: it should describe your procedure and the methods you used. Remember the rule that research should be repeatable: ideally, you should provide enough information so that someone else could repeat your research plan if they wanted to.

You should be able to draw on your work for Assignment 4 for this section.

5   *Statement of results*

This section is about what you found out as a result of your investigation. It is therefore a very important section. As Bell says, you may want to use tables or charts to summarise your findings: look back at your work for Unit 11 to get some ideas.

6   *Analysis and discussion*

Another important section, which explains how the results you achieved relate to the question or problem with which you began. This is also the place to talk about things that did not work as you expected, and to discuss why this may have happened.

7   *Summary and conclusions*

A brief summary of the main conclusions discussed in Section 6 above. Remember to include only statements for which you can provide evidence.

This is one of the sections that readers will turn to if they want a brief account of what your research is about.

8   *List of references*

Whether you provide a bibliography, list of references or both, this is where the bibliographical cards you have been compiling will prove their worth.

9   *Abstract*

You may also be asked to provide an abstract, which should be a very brief statement of your aims, methods and results. This usually goes at the beginning of the report but is written last.

You will find more information on this, and a sample abstract, on page 154 in Bell.

Features of an academic report

Once again, if you are following an investigation out of interest or perhaps as part of your work, not all of these features may be relevant to you. However, most of them are standard features, or designed to make your report easier to follow, so you may find them well worth including.

Bell includes the standard features which most reports will contain on pages 153–159, under the heading 'The Mechanics of Presenting a Report'. I have added a few comments on particular features below, including some which she doesn't mention here.

Title page

You will probably have guidelines as to what this should contain and how it should be laid out, if you are a student. If not, look at other similar reports for ideas.

Acknowledgements and thanks

Your chance to say ' Thank you' to the people who helped you in your research.

Headings

Headings help your readers to navigate through the sections of the report.

In a long report, it is a good idea to include a table of contents, listing the main sections or chapters and the pages on which they begin. You will obviously have to wait until the final version before you can prepare this, but a draft version, based on your outline, will help you to find your way around the report while it is being written.

Tables and figures

You will find lots of examples of both in Chapter 11 in Bell, together with one possible solution to the problem of numbering them. You will probably find it easiest to keep diagrams and charts, together with any other illustrations such as drawings or photographs, on pages separate from the text, unless you are using a very sophisticated method of production. If you number them, it will make it easy to refer to a particular example in your text.

Quotations

Follow the guidelines Bell gives on setting out quotations, and any 'house' rules. If you have not been given guidelines, writing longer quotations without quotation marks, as in the example on page 159 in Bell, is probably simpler.

Appendices

The appendices should include one (blank) copy of any questionnaires, interview schedules or other tools that have been used in your research.

The appendix is also the place for any other item to which you wish to refer, perhaps at several points during the report, which is too long to include in the body of the text. For example, if you were investigating the impact of a piece of legislation, you might want to include a copy of the law, or at least the most important clauses, as an appendix to your report.

Particularly if you are preparing your report for an academic award, it is a good idea to look at similar reports, prepared by fellow students at your institution or elsewhere, to give yourself an idea of how they are arranged, and what the different features look like. If you are preparing your report for an organisation, you may also be able to look at other reports produced for the same organisation which will give you an idea of the sort of layout and features that are expected.

Use these sample reports to check out any feature about which you are uncertain. For example:

- If there is a table of contents, how is it arranged?
- How long is the abstract, and what sort of detail does it contain?
- What sorts of things are placed in the appendices?
- How are the references presented?
- What about the overall layout – is it clear to follow, or cramped and confusing?

You may well find examples of techniques or features to avoid, as well as ones that you can use as models!

3 Stages of writing your report

The actual job of writing a report can be divided into stages. The ones I am going to discuss here are:

- Outlining
- Drafting
- Revising and editing
- Presentation.

Outlining

You may already have completed this stage, if you have been using index cards or loose sheets of paper to structure and rearrange your notes, as I suggested in Unit 3.

Use your notes or cards to draw up a detailed outline for the report, section by section.

The aim should be to have the structure of the report, and the relationship between the different sections, clear in note form.

Drafting

This is the stage at which you expand your notes or outline into a continuous written account. Once again, you may have completed drafts as you went along.

This is probably the most difficult part of the writing phase, so remember your writing plan and your techniques for avoiding procrastination.

Unless you are using a word processor, it is a good idea to write each paragraph of your first draft on a separate page, so that you can change the order, and add or remove bits, later. An alternative 'low technology' method is to cut and paste, or use arrows, to indicate changes in the order of paragraphs.

Assignment 5

When you have completed a first draft of your report, containing all the major sections in order (but not necessarily final tasks like the abstract and table of contents), send a copy to your tutor for comments. (Your tutor will not provide an analysis of *content* but will comment on your ways of approach.) If your schedule allows, wait until you have a reply before you start editing your report. This is a good idea for other reasons, as explained below.

Revising and editing

Bell has firm views on the need for revising and rewriting. You may feel that you do not have time to do as much redrafting as she suggests, but read what she has to say in any case.

Reading

Read the section 'The Need for Revision' in Chapter 12 in Bell (pages159–161). I would certainly agree that it is a good idea to put your draft aside for a few days if you can, so that you can come back to it with a fresh eye. If you wait until you receive comments on your first draft from your tutor, you will also be able to take note of these when you edit.

Check spelling, grammar, sequence, consistency as you read through. If you have access to a microcomputer with a word processing program, and know or can learn how to use it, I think you will find it a marvellous tool for redrafting and editing your report. Perhaps I am prejudiced, because I can no longer imagine writing anything without one, but I have also seen the almost magical transformation which it can produce in the quality of students' work. If like me you are an inaccurate typist, it makes correction easy, and if you are uncertain of your spelling, a program with a spelling checker can help with this too. Some programs come with a built-in thesaurus, and there are even grammar checking programs which will tell you if you use split infinitives or a singular verb with a plural subject.

But of course all this is very far from essential. Whatever method you choose for redrafting, the main thing is to be clear. As Bell says, remember as you read through your draft that whatever structure you have selected, your readers will need to be quite clear on:

- why you carried out the investigation
- how you conducted it
- what methods you used to gather your evidence
- what you found out.

I wonder what you thought about the story of the interview with the famous economist in Bell. If you are writing up a project to a tight schedule, this may sound like an impossible counsel of perfection. You may not need five drafts to achieve an acceptable result, and you are unlikely to have the time, or the resources, to be quite so cavalier with your earlier efforts! But the story is a useful reminder of the value of rewriting, even for people who are very experienced researchers.

Do try to get someone else to read your final draft, as Bell suggests, if you possibly can.

Presentation

Bell has a short section on presenting your report on page 159, and in the last paragraph before the checklist on page 163. Read these again now.

There is also a very useful list of questions for evaluating your report on page 162, which you should use to make certain that you have not forgotten anything.

Activity 5

When you have reached what you hope will be the final draft stage, check your report against the list of questions at the end of Chapter 12 in Bell (on page 162), before you write or type the final copy or send the final draft to the typist.

THE FINAL PRESENTATION

4 A final word

As Judith Bell does, I shall leave the last word to Daphne Johnson, who reminds us of the debt we as researchers owe to our subjects, and to those who provide us with the information we need. The basic rule of good researching is not to make things more difficult for those who come after us. How good an ambassador for your discipline are you?

If files are left in disarray, papers borrowed and not returned, or respondents subjected to too lengthy or frequent interviews, at inconvenient times, the researcher's welcome will be worn out. All social researchers are to some extent mendicants, since they are seeking a free gift of time or information from those who are the subject of study. But researchers who bear this fact in mind, and who, without becoming the captive of their respondents, can contrive to make the research experience a helpful and profitable one, will almost certainly be gratified by the generosity with which people will give their time and knowledge.

(Johnson 1984:11; quoted in Bell, pages 165–166)

5 Checklists

Chapter 12 in Bell has in effect two checklists, a general one to take you through the process of writing, and a special checklist to use when you go through the final draft (page 162). They are both full of valuable advice, and I recommend again that you use them as guides to carry you through the writing stage.

6 Suggested reading

There are so many books, of various kinds, on writing reports, that this is doomed to be a biased and incomplete sample.

Throughout the course, there have been references in Bell to a variety of texts which offer guidance on doing research, and many of these will have at least a chapter on writing up. You will find them all listed in the references at the end of the book and I have added some at the end of this course. Both Cohen and Manion (1989) and Coolican (1990) are worth special mention as guides for conducting and writing up social research projects.

Two from my own bookshelf that I have found useful may be worth mentioning: Bruce Cooper's *Writing Technical Reports* (1964) still offers lively and practical advice for technical writers despite its age, and *How to Write Effective Reports* by John E. Sussams (1983) is aimed at managers.

Finally, NEC offers a course by Roger Lewis and John Inglis (2nd edn 1991), *Report Writing: the Key to Successful Reports*, which takes you through the stages of preparing a report in detail, with lots of examples to give you practice.

References

This is a list of references, in the sense described in Unit 12: that is, a list of books and articles actually cited in this course. Texts which appear in the references section of the course text, Judith Bell (1993), *Doing Your Research Project* (Milton Keynes, Open University Press) are not included.

The list therefore includes two categories of references:

1   texts cited in the University of Sheffield course *Methods of Educational Enquiry*, written by Judith Bell, which are mentioned in this course but not cited in Bell (1993)

2   Additional references by the compiler of this course.

Borg, Walter R. (1963). *Educational Research: an Introduction*. New York, Longman.

Cooper, Bruce M. (1964). *Writing Technical Reports*. Harmondsworth, Penguin.

Hammond, Ray (1984). *The On-line Handbook*. Aylesbury, Fontana.

Lewis, Roger, and Inglis, John (1991). *Report Writing*. 2nd edn, Cambridge, National Extension College.

McNeill, Patrick (1990) *Research Methods*. 2nd edn, London, Routledge.

Mills, C. Wright (1970). *The Sociological Imagination*. Harmondsworth, Penguin.

Simons, Helen (1979). 'Classroom Action Research Network: School-based Evaluation', *Cambridge Institute of Education*, Spring 1979, 49–55, (reproduced in abridged form in Bell *et al.* (1984).

Sussams, John E. (1983). *How to Write Effective Reports*. Aldershot, Wildwood House.

Thouless, Robert H., and Christopher R. (1990). *Straight and Crooked Thinking*. London, Hodder and Stoughton.

COURSE COMMENTS

Course title _____

Course number _____

We would like to know what you think of this course and of any ideas you have for its improvement. Please write your comments on this page and send it to:

The Course Editor, NEC, 18 Brooklands Avenue, Cambridge CB2 2HN

Name _____

Student number _____

Address _____

_____

_____